.... Goz & Jason: I love your chwee kueh, your
goodness ...but most of all I love your BALLS!
for the tasty singaporean awesomeness — delish!
y xxx
cies.   OMG! Wow! Just like Singapore only better! - Lyall

CHWEE KUEH
IS THE
BOMB ☆
cheers to a geek
national day Pinrel.
yenyer

lagi sedap!
XO
suqave
x1
Kthanxba

This is 100% FACT!
I want it for breakfast
every day!
Oli

first
porean
lub experience.
thanks!
CA3 + Mike

FINALLY THE DAY HAS (
I HAVE TRIED SINGAPO
FOOD FOR THE 1ST
& I HAVE MET GO
GREAT NIGHT!! (
see you again s
HULA

wee fresh
ime! Yummi! Kelly
Delicious!
Thankyou!

Wot he said, (and they sa
This meal was FIT!
Thanks for an awesom
feed! Andy @jam!

Great supper club!!
Everything is great!
so stuffed. I don't
know how to make it
home! Thanks for cooking!
Elva

ved all
really home
vent Garden
that far!
Mei Ling

Blore
Amazing - Great
Succeed Cueh -
Cewioh Dard can +
compete. Thank
so much!
Chel

Fab- particularly
Otoh & Puk Bal
Yum.
B

OR, HOW TO SUBVERT SINGAPOREAN CULINARY MISCONCEPTIONS, AVERT STIR-FRY CALAMITIES, MAKE YOUR NYONYA GRANDMOTHER WEEP WITH JOY AND OTHER BADASS KITCHEN SKILLS.

Pork Belly Satay
PORK . SATAY SPICES . SKEWERS . FLAWLESS VICTORY.

CHWEE KUEH
RICE CAKES. CHILLI. PRESERVED TURNIP. A TYPICAL SINGAPOREAN BREAKFAST OF CHAMPIONS. TASTIER THAN WEETABIX.
CHEERIOS.
AND YO MOMMA IN THE MORNING.

ANNA HANSEN OF MODERN PANTRY LIKED IT SO YOU ARE A SILLY DODOFACE IF YOU DON'T.

LAKSA
THIS IS THE REAL DEAL. NOT THAT SLIME YOU GET AT SHITSU OR WHACKGANANA. EATEN WITH A SPOON COS THAT'S HOW REAL
KIDS DO IT.

BABI PONGTEH
AUTHENTIC PERANAKAN STYLE STEW. HANDED DOWN THE GENERATIONS LIKE A SECRET SCROLL OF NINJA SKILLS.
BE WORRIED IF YOU SCARED OF TASTY FOOD. COS THIS WILL CHUCK NORRIS ROUNDHOUSE KICK YOUR TASTEBUDS IN.

TEOCHEW BRAISED DUCK
GOZ HATES THIS DISH BECAUSE IT REMINDS HIM OF THE TIME HE WENT TO HAW PAR VILLA - SINGAPORE'S (AND PROBABLY THE
WORLD'S) ONLY THEME PARK ABOUT HELL. YES HELL. (ASK A SINGAPOREAN AROUND YOU OR GOOGLE IT IF YOU ARE AN ANTISOCIAL
DICK)

CHAP CHYE
A STIR FRY ON STERIODS. CHICKEN PRAWN STOCK. YELLOW BEAN PASTE. PORK CHEEKS. DAIKON. ALL KINDS OF MUSHROOMS AND
CRAZY TOFU BEANCURD MILK SKINS. OOOOH. SO. SO. HORNY.

CASSAVA CAKES
IT LOOKS LIKE ROAST PORK. I THINK.

SERVED
WITH A SIDE OF NOSTALGIA
&
HORRIBLY CHEESEY '80S MUSIC.
IT IS MANDATORY TO SING ALONG LOUDLY IF YOU KNOW THE SONG.

ESTD. LONDON 2011

PLUSIXFIVE

六五

A SINGAPOREAN SUPPER CLUB COOKBOOK

GOZ LEE AND FRIENDS

Designed by Shu Han Lee

EPIGRAM BOOKS / SINGAPORE

Designed by Shu Han Lee; plusixfive identity by SBTG

Photographs on pages ii–iii, 6, 10–11, 12, 15, 17, 20, 176, 188 and 243
published with permission of the author.

Photo Credits: Rachel Balota p 179: bottom right; Rory Daniel/Burnt Ends p 233;
Edible Experiences pp 29, 55, 82, 85, 95, 225, 236; Ming Tang Evans pp vi–1, 30;
HK Epicurus p 179: top left, Grace Hui pp 87, 246; Jason Michael Lang/Yardbird p 187;
Goz Lee pp 9, 35, 59, 69, 75, 90–91, 97, 135, 147, 155, 160, 164, 191, 195, 196,
219, 221, 227, 228–229, 235, 239, 240, 245, 248–249, backs of endpapers;
Shian Yuen Lee p 22; Wendy Lee-Warne p 141; Janice Leung Hayes p 179: bottom left;
Charmaine Mok p 179: top right, 183; Jocelyn Oye p 56; Edward Smith p 33;
Shuwen Tan p 81; Nicholas Tse pp 131, 213

Illustration credits: Goz Lee pp 14, 22, 32, 53, 57, 69, 70, 84, 90, 117, 142, 161, 165,
177, 214, 237, 238, 241, 244; Jason Ng p 136; Ken Sum pp vi, 87; Shuwen Tan p 80

These recipes were originally published in slightly different form in the
following places: Rice, as 'In Search of the Perfect Bowl of Rice', in *Crumbs*,
www.crumbsmag.com; Bak Kwa, as 'Bak Kwa – Sticky Smoky Salty-Sweet
Barbecue Meat Jerky', in *Great British Chefs*, www.greatbritishchefs.com;
Mui Choy Kong Bak, as 'Fennel and Preserved Mustard Greens with Slow
Soy Braised Pork Belly' in *Great British Chefs*, www.greatbritishchefs.com;
Chinese Pork Belly Satay, in *The Cork News*

National Library Board, Singapore Cataloguing-in-Publication Data

Lee, Goz.
Plusixfive : a Singaporean supper club cookbook / Goz Lee and Friends ;
designed by Shu Han Lee. – Singapore : Epigram Books, 2013.
pages cm

ISBN : 978-981-07-5906-3 (paperback)
ISBN : 978-981-07-5907-0 (ebook)

1. Cooking, Singaporean.

TX724.5.S55
641.595957 –- dc23 OCN 857379268

First Edition
10 9 8 7 6 5 4 3 2 1

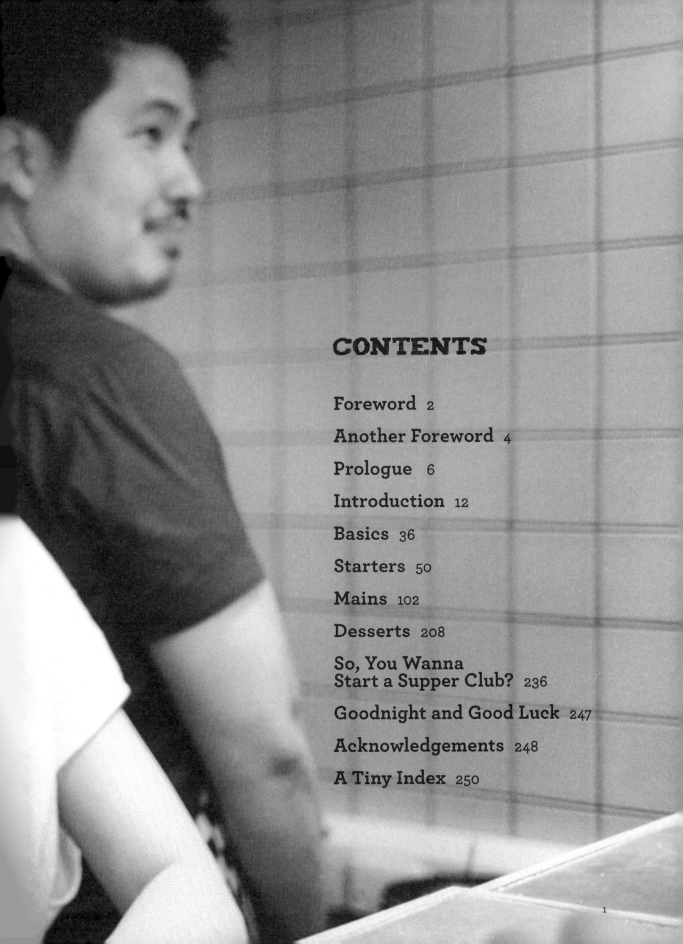

CONTENTS

We were supper club virgins and plusixfive took our virginity away from us.

Before our first visit, we had no idea what we were getting ourselves into, or the sheer amount of friends we were about to make...

It was our chef friend James Lowe who first told us about Goz and his supper club. He said, "You should go. They're very cute". Another gourmand friend, who was a frequent attendee, then convinced us to go.

We remember walking from Angel tube station, feeling very uncomfortable about dining at a stranger's home. But when we were about a block away from Goz's flat, we could smell the aromas coming out of the windows, which Goz and his friends had to leave open in order not to suffocate everyone inside. For Sandia, the smells of home cooking instantly brought back memories of comfort from her mother's cooking in the kitchen.

The atmosphere at Goz's dinners resembles that of a college reunion at a friend's house which is just big enough to fit everyone cosily. People arrive pulling bottles out of their bags, brandishing wine, cases of beers, magnum bottles of sake and secret stashes of strange liquors. You always make friends. Even if you don't like making friends, you don't have a choice! There's something about great food and the stories behind the food that make even the strangest strangers become peas in a pod. And its not just any stories that accompany each course, but Goz's extremely animated and Muppet-filled stories. Yes, Muppets are often involved at these dinners.

Then all of a sudden you find yourself surrounded by meticulously hand-crafted, delicious food, bathed in memories of Goz's childhood and those of your tablemates. Tips are shared, ideas are traded and recipes are given. The next thing you know, you're passing the rice down the table to your new-found friends, sharing the last piece of braised pork with the one-time stranger next to you, discussing ideas for your own restaurant, and planning the next time you can return.

On the walk back to Angel tube station, we smile. We smile because our tummies are full of wonderful food. We smile because someone has just shared his home with us. And we smile because we've just been forced to watch an hour of *The Muppets* on YouTube before we were allowed to go home, and we loved it. Plusixfive and its food have made us a lot of friends.

Sandia Chang & James Knappett
Co-owners, Bubbledogs& (London)

Hungry Singaporeans abroad are often driven to do some crazy things.

They make their own bak kwa or barbecued pork, a delicacy most people buy in shops. They turn to mothers, grandmothers, aunts or Google to find the perfect recipe for laksa. They develop repetitive strain injuries while scraping steamed rice flour cakes out of little metal moulds in order to make chwee kueh. These hot, wobbly cakes are then topped with preserved radish cooked, preferably, in lard, and are the sort of snack most sane people eat in hawker centres dotted around the island of Singapore. Overseas Singaporeans also find themselves skewering beef, mutton, chicken or pork to make satay, another popular hawker snack. They even make their own mooncakes, these crazy, homesick people.

Goz Lee and his gung-ho buddies have gone a step further. They have formed a supper club in London called plusixfive, a reference to the international calling code of Singapore, to share their joy in and passion for the food they grew up eating. By cooking for groups of people they have never met, they have helped to spread the word about the gutsy, pungent, aromatic and just plain delicious food we eat on this tiny island. In their own way, they have put Singaporean food on the world map.

And now, they have collected their recipes in this funny, irreverent book. This is not a solemn tome on the correct way to make classic Singaporean dishes. It is filled with stories, anecdotes and secret recipes they have developed over the years, with contributions from people they have met, cooked for and dined with.

Wherever you are in the world, whether you are Singaporean or not, you might just be inspired enough to get into the kitchen and start banging those pots and pans about, to create meals that people halfway across the world relish every day.

Goz and gang—there is method in their madness.

Tan Hsueh Yun
Food Editor, *The Straits Times*

ONE NIGHT IN A SUPPER CLUB COOKBOOK

I suppose I can be described as obstinate, occasionally obsessive and always naive, especially when I latch onto an idea.

So when the mustard seed of a cookbook idea was planted, it slowly became the Moby Dick to my Ahab. One way or another, it just had to be done.

I decided that since this was a cookbook featuring recipes from the plusixfive supper club, it would only be apt for it to be a literary interpretation of a plusixfive dinner.

Held every fortnight on a Sunday, every supper club dinner follows roughly the same format. Once all the guests have arrived, drunk a little, comingled and made awkward attempts at introductions to fellow guests, hoping, cross-fingered, that they do not turn out to be serial murderers or worse, serial anti-socialites, we give a short introduction to the meal. Then we launch full-throttle into the dinner service, accompanied by anecdotes and memories, in our regular order of starters, mains and desserts.

Before anyone's inner traditionalist bursts out, waving flags, beating chests and crying out that this is not how Singaporean food is usually served, they should just stop and think about what Singaporean food really is. There isn't one traditional way of serving Singaporean food because the cuisine itself is a disparate amalgamation of at least three major ethnic cuisines: Indian, Malay and Chinese. Also, if you really want to get pedantic here, whenever you go to a hawker centre and sit there waiting for your big main meal to come along, be honest and ask yourself, how many times have you gone over to get a little snack from the popiah stall or the satay uncle? That pre-meal nibble is arguably a starter, no?

But the main reason for this arrangement is that during the gestational periods of plusixfive, I thought long and hard about what I wanted the format of the meal to be. Should it be a full-on, Singaporean Chinese-style meal where plates of food just get piled on the table as and when they are ready? Or should the meal have a formal structure? I had so many dishes in my head and I wanted to be able to showcase as much food as possible without overwhelming our guests. So, taking my cue from the degustation menus of smarter West End restaurants in London's Soho neighbourhood, I decided to serve mini nibbles as starters to whet everyone's appetite, before launching into the main courses and a few small desserts.

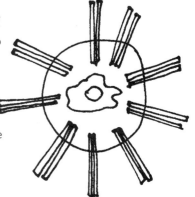

Also, everything—save for maybe plated desserts—would be shared. That was something that I insisted on.

Sharing has been my biggest bugbear in English food cultures, where the tendency is for everyone to order their own meal and not to share or try each other's mains.

Singapore is a nation where meal sharing is almost mandatory. Meals involving more than one person, especially large extended family dinners, always feature an assortment of dishes placed in the centre of the table, and everyone helps themselves. You don't have to choose. You just order everything on the menu.

And so, I wanted my guests to eat like I ate at home and get sharing.

Whilst we try to maintain a consistently high standard of cooking, I have always firmly believed that a plusixfive night should not be defined solely by its food. One of the main aims of the supper club was to share with Londoners what Singaporeans eat and hopefully through that, a little bit of the nostalgia for Singapore that we all share. So with every dish that comes out of the kitchen, we also serve up snatches of our memories of home, mostly from childhood, and how and why we were inspired to cook that particular dish. Although it did not begin as a conscious effort, the stories served as the garnishing on the dish, and sharing stories became an integral part of the plusixfive experience.

> **I want the guests to feel as if they are eating a feast at a friend's crib and not as if they are dining at a restaurant.**

As with any other supper club, chances are you'll be seated at a table with a random menagerie of personalities. We've had food critics, journos, train drivers, graphic designers, artists, gallery owners, doctors, bankers, lawyers, hairdressers, photographers and a heck of a lot of chefs come through our doors and share meals, drinks, banter and laughs with one another. You name the profession, we've probably served them. (We have not had millionaire drug lords or hookers yet though—or not that we know of anyway.)

I want the guests to feel as if they are eating a feast at a friend's crib and not as if they are dining at a restaurant. They should feel free to poke their noses into my open-plan kitchen and holler out for seconds; to grab me or any member of my team and grill us on how we made the dish so gawddamn tasty; to leave general dining etiquette at the door and feel unashamed to get elbow deep and messy peeling crab shells, sucking on prawn heads and fighting for the last piece of chwee kueh with a bunch of strangers they've just met. And after the dinner is done and I can finally relax, I want them all to linger, refusing to leave despite the fact that it's a school night. The team and I can then shake off our aprons, throw on some Massive Attack, sit down with the guests and, amidst piles of dirty crockery, share a nice stiff drink or two. Or ten.

And when the room is filled with the raucous nattering, laughter and banter of strangers who have met just hours before, drowning out the '80s synth lines and warbling vocals of The Killers in the background, I know that the night has been one awesomely successful plusixfive night.

Beyond being just a vanilla compendium of essential recipes, this book is also laced—like a dirty bowl of spicy tonkotsu ramen with all the works—with sexy snippets, delicious tales and filthy anecdotes from a few friends and me. I have also managed to ~~bribe~~ ~~arm-twist~~ ~~blackmail~~ persuade a few guests, helpers and others who have in some shape or form crossed paths with plusixfive, to contribute recipes to the book.

So as you read, I hope that with a teeny bit of help from your imagination, you will be transported to a nondescript, quiet little street in Angel, Islington, London, and follow your nose to a noisy little flat where, for one random Sunday evening, a little bit of Singapore is recreated from my wee kitchen.

THE BIRTH OF A BADASS SINGAPOREAN SUPPER CLUB

"Singapore? Huh? Wah?"

When I first went to the UK to study as a teenager, most people, when asked where Singapore was, would usually think it was somewhere in China and accordingly, that we ate the same dubious Oriental stuff they peddle in Camden Town, i.e. something along the lines of rice with a side of Sweet and Sour Gloopy Mystery Meat. Even when people knew where Singapore was, instead of being well known for our delectable cuisine, chances are, they probably knew Singapore as *the* country that banned chewing gum, fined you for not flushing, caned you if you doodled on walls, and jailed your ass if you gave blow jobs. God help you if you were doing all of the above.

here
yes here
see???

To me, not knowing about Singaporean food is like not knowing that the Incredible Hulk is green. We're a nation of food lovers—and that's an understatement. At any time of day, go to any part of Singapore and chances are, you can just about find whatever you're craving. And when Singaporeans aren't eating, we're talking about food, dissecting the meal we just had and discussing where the next meal should be. We get into arguments, monologues and long discourses defending our favourite dishes and hawkers and denouncing others. We have reams of pages in the newspapers devoted to food. We write songs about food, make movies and soap operas about food and have countless TV variety shows devoted to hunting down, reviewing, tasting, cooking, discussing and sourcing food. Hell, we even greet each other by asking if the other person has eaten.

Surely local food should be Singapore's greatest resource and export. Everyone knows about Vietnamese food, Indian food, Thai food and Malaysian food, but for some reason, Singapore has fallen off the international culinary radar.

When I first discovered 'Singapore Fried Noodles' after a night out in London, among the usual suspects on the grease-stained menu of a nondescript London Chinatown joint, I was ecstatic.

I thought I had found a truly authentic Singaporean noodle dish like char kway teow (for the uninitiated, this is a dish of thick noodles licked with fire as it stir-fries in a scorching hot wok with sweet dark soya sauce and savoury chunks of Chinese chorizo; the oily richness of it all sliced right through with the metallic piquancy of raw blood cockles) or even better, bak chor mee (flat egg noodles tossed in a rich pork broth and mixed with a heavily seasoned combination of minced pork and mushrooms, generously drizzled with tangy rice wine vinegar and lashings of sambal chilli). Instead, dumped before me was a plate of radioactively luminous yellow noodles punctuated by commas of limp shredded pork, a feeble whimper of scrambled eggs and a mess of some unidentifiable vegetable.

I knew then that something had to be done. And so it was, that against this backdrop, the rumbling seeds of a Singaporean supper club were first planted.

Not Quite a Five Point Palm Exploding Heart Technique

At that point, the supper club was still a pretty long way from being anything but a fleeting idea. Mainly because back then, I had all the culinary skills of an awkward, pimply, skirt-chasing teenager in a pre-Jamie Oliver age, when cooking just wasn't the sexy rock-star scene it is today, i.e. I had no idea how to cook save for maybe turning on the kettle to fix up a cup of instant noodles.

People always ask how I learnt to cook the dishes that I churn out at plusixfive. I would love to be able to stare wistfully into the distance and tell them dog-eared sepia tales of times gone by when I sat in the kitchen as a child absorbing everything my grandma did and being taught every step ala Karate Kid's 'wax on wax off' style, slowly graduating from the lowly tasks of scrubbing her pestle and mortar to hand-chopping turnip for popiah to finally attaining culinary nirvana, channelling Bruce Lee's 'feel, don't think' mantra and instinctively and effortlessly making each kueh pie tee shell with a flick of the wrist.

But this couldn't be further from the truth, even though I did spend most of my childhood helping my mum and granny out in the kitchen. The first thing I learnt, from the many years of teary onion eyes and garlicky fingers after helping them finely dice the basis for just about every meal they made, was the holy trinity of garlic, shallots and ginger. And then helping them stir-fry that until fragrant before they took over, adding in the other ingredients. That has definitely stuck with me to this very day.

But I am ashamed to say that unfortunately (and, I dare say, like most Singaporeans), I never really saw the need to learn every dish they made. I took it all for granted. It was there whenever I needed it. If there was anything else I craved, I could just pop into any hawker centre and find a smorgasbord of culinary brilliance at practically any time of day. Why the hell would I bother learning how to cook?

In fact, one of the first dishes I cooked on my own involved buying frozen pre-packed sausage rolls from 7-11, lobbing them into the microwave and jabbing the buttons corresponding to the instructions on the flimsy packet. At the age of 13, a few friends and I also went to the local supermarket

after school and picked up a couple of cans of spaghetti and frankfurters. Yes, that's right. Spaghetti. In a can. We went home, turned up the gas stove, dunked them into a gigantic pot and waited for it all to come to a messy, greasy, mushy boil. But of course in between watching Ninja Turtles on the telly and playing Digger on my 486 computer, we completely and utterly forgot about it. It burnt the bottom of the pot and we ended up eating tomatoey, carbony mush and then spent the next hour taking turns to scrape the mess from the pot. Sorry, Mum.

It was Jamie Oliver's *Naked Chef* television series that made me sit up and realise how easy it was to cobble together dishes I had previously thought impossible to make at home. His cavalier fashion of cooking was reminiscent of the way my grandmother and mother cooked—it was always a pinch of this and a drizzle of that. He rarely, if ever, took out weighing scales or measuring cups. It was all about tasting and touching and feeling the food. This spurred me on to slowly venture into the kitchen and ask my mum to teach me the various basics of cooking and also to experiment with salads, pastas and Sunday roasts—dishes I had previously thought to be the domain of restaurants and chefs.

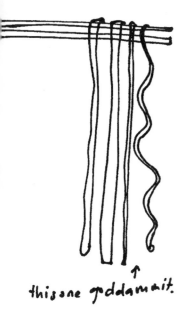

this one goddamit.

But it was only a few years later when necessity forced me to learn how to cook Singaporean food. That old proverb 'absence makes the heart grow fonder' really is true. I found this out the hard way when I returned to London in 2007 for work and realised that none of the restaurants in Chinatown could satiate my craving for good ol' Singaporean food. Even those claiming to serve 'Singaporean food' always fell slightly short of the real thing.

Laksa is a perfect example. Sometimes you get lucky. You hear about a place that just about gets the broth perfect. You sit down, order, gingerly dip your spoon into the bowl and savour the perfectly balanced, perfumed broth. You smile to yourself at the beginning of a potentially amazing meal and enthusiastically dig your chopsticks in.

Only to discover to your horror that they have used the WRONG NOODLES.

It's like spending ages devising and plotting the perfect bank robbery, only to use a broken second-hand tricycle as a getaway vehicle.

It was probably somewhere over my tenth unsatisfactory bowl of bad laksa, chewy, bone-dry satay or unforgivably tasteless Hainanese chicken rice that something inside me snapped and said, "To hell and mee siam with this! I'm going to stop complaining about how crap Singaporean food is in London and teach myself how to cook what I wanna eat when I wanna eat it!"

So I slowly started to experiment with cooking Singaporean food at home, learning from recipes off the Internet and exchanging emails with my mum asking for her methods and guidance. And the more I experimented and learnt, the more curious I was and the more hungry I got for more recipes. I just kept plugging away at it, trying out new dishes every weekend and perfecting older ones. I also started hosting dinner parties for my friends. I love hosting and having friends around and there's nothing more social than having everyone over feasting. Looking back, the dinner parties were also probably excuses for me to spur myself to cook better, as I received comments and criticism from my friends.

Once I started learning how to cook, I realised that even though all the recipes might have appeared daunting at first, once I peeled away my initial apprehension, there really wasn't any secret martial art move like some Five Point Palm Exploding Heart Technique. Everything was so gawddamn simple.

On the (Tudor) Road

Ben Greeno, now big-time head honcho of Momofuku Seiōbo, was chef-proprietor of the first supper club I ever went to—the Tudor Road supper club.

This was a time when the concept of supper clubs was still relatively novel and they were few and far between. The idea of going to a complete stranger's home to eat a meal with other complete strangers was counter-cultural to me, and if I'm honest, filled me with utter fear and loathing. What if my dining companions were Rohypnol-dispensing, kidney-farming murderers? What if the chef's inspiration was Sweeney Todd? Or worse, what if they were all just plain boring?

Arriving at Ben's, my friend Yen Lin and I were greeted by a long communal table and a pre-Twitter me sat next to a bunch of bloggers who introduced themselves by their Twitter handles like some strange superhero club: @hollowlegs, @lovelychaos and @tehbus. They were rambunctious and obnoxious, and could collectively talk the ears off a statue—and this was before they had even started drinking. Maybe it was something in the air that night, or the wine, or Ben Greeno's expertly executed cooking, but we hit it off almost immediately and have since remained in touch.

More importantly, the Tudor Road supper club showed me the possibility of starting a supper club in my own home and was the start of the slow

blossoming of plusixfive. Ben used his home as a platform for showcasing his own style of modern British cuisine, using the techniques and skills he picked up in restaurants like Momofuku Ko and Noma, and local British seasonal produce found in farmers' markets and foraged from local parks and gardens. Returning home, I couldn't stop jabbering away to Yen Lin, who had dragged me to the supper club, about the possibility of doing something similar. Only we would be showcasing the wide array of Singaporean food.

I had already been hosting regular dinners at mine for upwards of 12 to 14 friends and I had volunteered to cook for 60 people every Friday at church, so how much more difficult could it possibly be to host a supper club?

I dimly recalled the words of Anthony Bourdain, one of my heroes, ringing in my ear like an evil, brooding doomsayer. In one chapter of *Kitchen Confidential*, he rants that there is nothing stupider than someone opening a restaurant just because he thinks he can cook well and because his friends have always said, hey you cook so well, you should really open a restaurant! Ben Greeno had been one of the head pastry chefs at Noma and had an extensive and enviable CV at some of the top restaurants in the world. I was a full-time City lawyer who cooked on the weekends. Occasionally. Who the hell in their right mind would want to come eat at mine and *pay* me for that dubious honour?

More notably, I only knew how to cook. I was absolutely and utterly clueless about logistics, marketing, ticketing and all those generally boring administrative and accounting type things. To make matters worse, I was the equivalent of a technological sloth. I thought a hashtag referred to something you rolled in an Amsterdam coffee shop, and I owned a prehistoric dot matrix mobile phone, the most advanced technological feature of which could be found in its dim torchlight function. The logistics of running a supper club were all one big impenetrable, unnavigable miasma to me.

That's where Wen Lin came in. In a nutshell, we met, we bantered, we plotted, we schemed, brainstormed, bickered and bantered some more; I learnt about Twitter, hashtags and blogging, and after a couple of mini trial runs, we launched the first plusixfive supper club on 29 May 2011. We invited a couple of notable food bloggers, including those I had met at Tudor Road, and as the age-old adage goes, the rest is history.

This is Wen's slightly more loquacious and compelling account.

WEN LIN: My husband Amir and I were travelling around the Middle East in the autumn of 2009. Because Goz had done a trip in the region before, I emailed him asking for some food recommendations. I didn't know Goz very well at that point. We had been introduced by a mutual friend only

Who the hell in their right mind would want to come eat at mine and *pay* me for that dubious honour?

a few months before. I just knew Goz wasn't your average fellow because he'd decided to do his big Middle East trip (including Iran) alone, and he regularly took on rather strange food projects like making apple noodles, whatever that might be.

That didn't prepare me for the string of emails that came from him. Plenty of fabulous recommendations. Even more capital letters and exclamation marks. And when I (it would seem) failed to communicate adequate enthusiasm on certain points made, there were more emails and more capital letters.

Babs and I eventually moved on from the Middle East, but the emails with Goz continued. Mostly we argued about food and restaurants. The conversation continued when we got back to London. We talked. Incessantly. About feeling nostalgic for Singaporean food. About modern Singaporean food and our ambivalence about it. About old school Chinese calendars. About ice shavers. About supper clubs. About how to start one. About what to name his. What to do in the kitchen. What to do outside the kitchen.

At the time Amir and I were just starting to build Edible Experiences, an online hub for culinary activities. Our aim was to take care of the marketing, ticketing and payment woes faced by small, independent food-related ventures such as cooking schools and supper clubs, so that proprietors could focus on the food part of their business. So we figured a good arrangement would be for Goz to focus on cooking at plusixfive, and I would take care of the front of house, publicity and bookings, as first-hand research for building our website.

We had the original intention to seat eight guests at the debut plusixfive dinner in Goz's living room in May 2011. In the end we seated 10, many of whom were food bloggers we knew with some affectionate link to Singapore or Malaysia, who were dying for some authentic, homemade Singaporean food in London.

From there, word spread faster than we had dared to hope. One day someone emailed us to say they had seen us mentioned in *Time Out London*. After that it felt like a grenade had landed in plusixfive's inbox. Gradually a lot of my job became writing notes of apology that we couldn't seat so-and-so this time around...hopefully next time around...Goz and I absolutely hated telling people we couldn't feed them. We felt great and awful all at the same time.

With multiple rounds of furniture Tetris, plusixfive dinners grew until we could seat 18 guests and there was no more furniture that could be moved around. Every plusixfive dinner has been sold out since, even at supper club festivals, which sat between 30 to 50 guests at a go.

It's been a real privilege and honour to be part of the founding team of plusixfive, feeding Singaporean food to the homesick and curious alike, dispelling Singaporean food myths, converting a few lifestyle vegetarians via the magic of pork belly.

A new generation of 'ethnic cuisine' supper clubs blossomed in London after plusixfive, many of them similarly frustrated that London was a food desert, as far as authentic renditions of their native cuisines were concerned. Many of them, I am delighted to say, now work with Edible Experiences.

So, here's a toast to discovering great food finds in deserts, be they literal or figurative. And to more opportunities to help create these food oases.

All I wanted was for us to be the first and best, bigbadass, stupidest, nuttiest feeders of Singaporean food in town.

Kindness of Strangers

When I started plusixfive, all I wanted was for us to be the first and best, bigbadass, stupidest, nuttiest feeders of Singaporean food in town, serving up honest, awesome-as-hell, tastebud-kicking cuisine. I never thought about reviews or interviews.

So it's always nice (and sometimes I still have to pinch myself to believe it) when people take the time to post photos on the Internet and write about plusixfive. It's crazy that I didn't even have to bribe these people. Throughout

plusixfive's journey, the blogging world has been too kind. Plusixfive has even made it to mainstream news publications—a feature in *Time Out London*, a huge centre spread in the national financial newspaper of Singapore *The Business Times*, Malaysia's *New Straits Times*, UK's *Telegraph* online, Hong Kong's *South China Morning Post*, and Irelands' *The Cork News*. I have even been invited to be on panels and live television discussing the future of Singaporean hawker food. Craziness.

We are plusixfamily

As time went by, perceptions of Singaporean food seemed to change for each non-Singaporean supper clubber and hopefully for the Singaporean punter, a little bit of homesickness was assuaged with each sambal prawn head sucked and each kueh pie tee cup demolished. But it was only over a year into operations that I really started to see the impact of plusixfive. I began to see similar supper clubs popping up all over London, all of them dedicated to showcasing ethnic food and almost all of them stemming from a mis- or under-representation of such cuisine in London.

I knew then that it was time for plusixfive to expand. It had grown well past its infant stages into a brash and confident juvenile who was itching to go places and expand its horizons. Also, I knew that in the very near future, I would have to leave London and relocate to Hong Kong for work. And plusixfive at that point was really just me. Without me, the whole shindig would atrophy and disappear into the ether of time like some Singaporean supper club Keyser Söze.

Embracing the motto of Marvel Comics' fictional organisation of maximum villainy, Hydra—'If a head is cut off, two more will take its place'—I decided to actively keep an eye out for worthy people to take over the supper club, people who could continue the legacy of inspiring others to cook and celebrate Singaporean food with the same spirit in which I had created plusixfive.

My goal was ultimately to build an epicurean community around plusixfive: the plusixfamily. And in no time, thanks to the wonderful World Wide Web, I found just the right people.

Jason

I met Jason for the first time at another supper club, Wild Serai, which was run by my friend Yolanda and which I had helped to debut. Until then, all our conversations had happened on Twitter. Upon meeting Jason, I wondered how he'd managed to constrain himself to 140-character tweets because this dude could talk for England. I would slowly come to learn

My goal was ultimately to build an epicurean community around plusixfive: the plusixfamily.

that even when no one was talking to him, the dude would talk to himself, especially when he was in the kitchen, walking himself through each step of the cooking process while thinking aloud. He was a lyrical shark—his very survival seemed to depend on his constant soliloquy. In fact, in the months to come, whenever I didn't hear from him for more than 10 minutes, I would check up on him in the kitchen, just to see if he was all right. He was fine—he usually just had food in his mouth.

Jason was one intensely obsessed perfectionist. Not only did he have a website, *Feast to the World*, where he tried to recreate and painstakingly document all his grandmother's (or 'nan's') cooking, he also managed to somehow find time between his day job, constant eating out, incessant posting to Twitter and Instagram, to update his website nearly every other day with a new recipe, step-by-step photos and all the bells and whistles. Oh, and he also eschews the use of most modern-day equipment, preferring to mince or chop meat and vegetables by hand when most would settle for a mincer or a mandoline, and pounding rempah (spice paste) with a pestle and mortar when most would use a blender. (At one particular plusixfive dinner, we had to make laksa for over 30 people and he still insisted on pounding the rempah by hand with his tiny pestle and mortar. He also hand-minced the meat for the ngoh hiang for that same event. If that isn't dedication, I'm not sure what is.)

I knew I had quite possibly met my match in terms of being a crazed, obsessed, perfectionist-purist. And most importantly, I knew he was the perfect nut job candidate for the plusixfamily.

JASON: Almost all my childhood memories revolve around good food. My nan was a great cook and like most women of her generation, it was very important for her to feed her family well, and that was her way of showing her adoration. Day after day, she would get up at the crack of dawn to start the daily mammoth task of preparing the family meal. It was laborious work as various kinds of rempah would be painstakingly pounded to perfection under her watchful eye. Everything ran like clockwork in her kitchen and it was a fascinating sight for me as a child, still gradually learning about the importance of cooking. All I knew back then was that whatever she cooked tasted wonderful and I wanted more.

My fascination soon evolved into a deep passion for wanting to know what went into the mortar and what each rempah was used for, how to transform something as humble as belacan, shallots, garlic and chillies into all these delicious dishes that landed on our dining table. I've been

> **Most importantly, I knew Jason was the perfect nut job candidate for the plusixfamily.**

very fortunate to have most of these skills handed down to me from my nan through years of cooking alongside her as I was growing up. Along with traditional Peranakan delights such as babi pongteh, popiah and countless varieties of kueh, she also made dishes from other cuisines like ayam biryani, Hainanese chicken rice and bak kut teh. These recipes were acquired through her lifelong, non-stop pursuit of good food and begging, borrowing or stealing from the many culinary heroes she met along the way.

After years of being thousands of miles away from these familiar dishes, I was determined to recreate and share my grandma's many wonderful recipes. I began the journey by writing a food blog. This led me to stumble upon the world of supper clubs, and more specifically, plusixfive.

My very first visit to plusixfive was on fish head curry night. Although slightly sceptical at first, I was gleefully surprised by the array of familiar food. These weren't your average bastardised affairs, instead it was food made with authenticity and conviction. As I got to know Goz, I came to admire his ambition and determination to promote Singaporean cuisine, something that I was trying to achieve with my own blog. Subsequently, he asked me to collaborate with him on a few supper club events, and I've been cooking as part of the plusixfive team ever since.

For this cookbook, I've chosen recipes that have been served throughout the supper club. More importantly, they're dishes that are very close to my heart—a legacy of my culinary hero and muse, my nan.

These weren't your average bastardised affairs, instead it was food made with authenticity and conviction.

Shu Han

"Hello, I'm a fellow Singaporean here and chanced upon this from an old post by Hollow Legs. I have been boasting to everyone I know in London about the super good food in singapore, this supper club sounds like an awesome way to prove my point, congrats on taking the plunge to start this- I love cooking and have always played around with that idea myself but I share a studio with a friend and as it is we have hardly any walking space- and good luck with future dinners! the menu looks mouth-wateringly good and I would have definitely gone for the national day dinner - if not for the fact that i'm back in Singapore for summer and have been enjoying the very same things HUR HUR HUR. anyway, will be keeping an eye on this, drop by my blog too if you like, and do lmk of future events (may be a little hard on my own meagre-stdudent-budget pocket but I can definitely spread the news to my friends!). once again, amazing job, so super jealous but so super happy for you all too!"

Shu Han had either mastered the ability to bend the space-time continuum or was one insanely talented food-obsessed crazy.

Those were the first words Shu Han said to me. Or rather, those were the first words she left as a comment on an article I wrote online, warts (typographical, grammatical, punctuation errors) and all.

As a creepy, seasoned online stalker, I managed to find her blog, *Mummy, I Can Cook!*, and it was love at first click. This was a university student who had somehow, over the course of a year or so, singlehandedly compiled a compendium of recipes of Singaporean food often tied in with British seasonal produce, and her blog was gorgeously designed with minimal fuss and clean lines. How she managed to cook, document, experiment and photograph all these dishes while completing a design degree at Central Saint Martins, managing Pimlico Farmers Market on the weekends and juggling a bunch of other freelance jobs on the side boggled me. She had either mastered the ability to bend the space-time continuum or was one insanely talented food-obsessed crazy. Either way, I knew I had to convince her to be part of plusixfive.

SHU HAN: My mum is a wonderful cook. You would think this means her kids all grew up brandishing woks and slicing onions without a tear in their eyes. Unfortunately, my sisters, brother and I were not quite the culinary prodigies you would expect. You see, my mother was fiercely protective of her kitchen. It was her space, her divine territory, where she did her 'thing', and we, mere little imps, were not allowed to mess up this sacred part of the house with our amateur attempts at cooking. I may just be a bit bitter on hindsight—because frankly, it's much more likely that she (like most Asian mothers) just wanted her children to be free from menial distractions, so we could spend our time hitting the books or playing the piano.

So I found myself pretty much thrown into the deep end when I went to London to study, with nothing but a handful of skills scraped together from hazy memories of secondary school Home Economics class, and my mum's worried Skype conversations. I didn't succumb to instant noodles though, and was very proud of my (at least edible) meals. In fact, I loved it. It's hard not to get excited about food growing up in a country with a fiery hawker culture and a house with a fiery cook of a mum. And here in London, I continue to get excited about food, especially after finding the best part-time job in the world—managing a farmer's market in London—where I find myself happily surrounded by the smell of fresh bread and the colours of vegetables in their myriad seasonal hues (albeit too early on a Saturday morning). But it was when I discovered the joy of making this food myself that things got really exciting for me. I've turned into a cross between an 'auntie' and a geek: fascinated by cooking shows, cookbooks and food-related conversations, and stubbornly inspired by my own failures in the kitchen.

I never thought I would one day be cooking dinners for 18 (or even 50), or that I would be writing about food and have readers, but I guess the world has a funny way of making things happen in the most incredible way. I started blogging about the food I make and love, using food that's grown locally with love and the comforting flavours and bold spices of home. Goz read my blog and decided, "We need to meet at the nearest pub. NOW". I turned down his offer because it was almost midnight and this stranger was too scarily enthusiastic, but after a rainy afternoon meeting at Monmouth with this strangely convincing ball of energy, I found myself at a plusixfive supper club for the first time and, quite dauntingly, thrown straight into the kitchen. To my relief, the guests seemed to not hate the sambal, I didn't break Goz's Le Creuset, and upon his nagging and prodding, I even found myself cooking for the next supper club...and the next...and the next...

In addition to Jason and Shu Han, a whole host of other amateur cooks and hungry friends have passed through the plusixfamily and been eager

contributors and participants, including, most notably, the lovely fashion journalist Christine, who has joined the ranks as the main front of house, occasional chef and permanent man tou bun maker.

If there was ever a culinary version of the X-Men (although that does not make me a folically challenged, wheelchair-bound, psychic mutant), I am positive the plusixfamily is pretty close to it. Some members of the family have been inspired to start their own supper clubs and some have gone to culinary school, but all have remained firm friends who I know I can count on if I flick on the Bat (or should it be Fat?) Signal for any last-minute help.

You Say You Want (R)evolution?

In 2013 plusixfive entered the age of the terrible twos. And true to the personality of a curious, feisty, tantrummy two-year-old, we were itching for more. The concept of a supper club held in a home just wasn't enough, so we started venturing out, evolving and trying out new things.

And when we ventured out of our comfort zones, we sure didn't just take little baby steps. We did offsite catering gigs—the most notable being for Contact Singapore, where we were asked to cater dinner at an event that was attended by the Singapore High Commissioner to London!

We are also grateful to Yum Bun for agreeing to collaborate with us. Yum Bun, one of the true rock stars of the London street food scene, famous for their pork belly buns that are akin to our Singaporean kong bak pau, have managed to grow from their humble beginnings at Exmouth Market to a bricks-and-mortar shop in Old Street. There, we dished out over a hundred of our versions of their famous buns—one with popiah filling and another with beef rendang.

Back in the Far East, in Hong Kong, we were invited to set up a stall in a local artisanal food market where we whipped up bowls of steaming hot laksa, juicy rendang buns, and delectable Mexican-Peranakan-inspired tacos.

I'm not quite sure what else the future holds, but I am pretty sure it's gonna be pretty darn fun and delicious.

Lazy Sonofa—! (Or 'Why We Should All Learn How to Cook')

I really don't believe people when they say they can't cook. I do believe people can be lazy however, and I don't mean this in a 'you lazy sonofa—!' derogatory manner at all. Most people who say they can't cook, simply just can't be arsed to. In Singapore, there is even *less* of an incentive to learn because the ability to feed your face is just a stone's throw away at any one of the thousands of hawker centres littered throughout the country.

Well, here's why we should all learn how to cook: take a walk around the nation's hawker centres and you will hardly be greeted by scenes of spritely eager beaver teenagers with a gummiberry bounce in their steps who have woken up at 4am that day to wash and grind soya beans to make your favourite silky smooth tau hway (soya bean curd) for breakfast, or gleefully, skilfully flipping roti prata on a ghee-smeared hot pan. Chances are, most, if not all, of the stalls are run by po-faced, leathery-skinned, weather-beaten, ashen-haired geriatrics. And give or take another 10 years, unless we come up with some miracle drug for immortality, these stalls will fade into the ashes of time, reduced to nothing more than a mere mention on someone's blog or a footnote in some culinary historian's unpublished thesis. And along with that, all the recipes, skills and know-how that go into that favourite dish of yours.

You may not even have to wait that long. With inflation, rising rents and food costs, some of those geriatrics have made the difficult decision of closing shop. Some have sold their businesses or handed them over to others. Those hawkers with kids have either forbidden their kids from taking over, thinking, "Why the hell did I work so hard as a hawker to put you through

university just so you could be a hawker too?" or, more likely the case, the kids themselves have no interest in taking over such a laborious business with low financial returns, after seeing what their parents had to go through.

I am back at one of my favourite tze char stalls in Bukit Timah market after a couple of years' absence. You can find whole sweet and sour deep-fried seabass at just about any self-respecting tze char stall in Singapore, but you would be hard-pressed to find a good black bean deep-fried version of it. I remembered eating it there growing up when I used to live nearby at my grandma's. When I went back this time however, the stall was still there but the seabass was not on the menu any more. The old Hainanese man said that people had stopped ordering the black bean version, so he took it off the menu. We ordered a few of his other dishes, and although they were still far better than any other tze char I've had, it just was not as good as I remembered. Then I caught his eye and realised, the passion was gone. He was resigned and tired. Not just from the day's hard work but just plain tired of it all; the daily humdrum, the rising rental costs and the everyday pressures of life had gotten to him. He was just going through the motions and trying to earn a living and get by.

When I dropped by the stall at Old Airport Road market selling otak otak, a fragrant fish paste wrapped in banana leaves and grilled over charcoal, I asked the lady behind the counter what fish she used and where I could find the leaves too. She stared at me blankly as if I had asked her to explain the meaning of life in Hebrew and replied, "How I know? All make in factory one lah!"

Even my old coffee shop haunt selling kaya toast has stopped making their own kaya, instead they are using kaya from an industrial-sized tin, presumably all made in the same grey factory. And at a wholesaler where I was buying preserved turnip in bulk to bring back to Hong Kong in order to make chwee kueh for our first pop-up market stall, the lady asked me quizzically why I'd wanted to make the topping myself. She thrust a pack of vacuum-packed, premade chwee kueh topping at me, gesturing at the hawker centre behind, saying the guys there used it if I wanted to go taste test it first.

Before a Peranakan stall I used to frequent shut down, the owner had told me that people just were not willing to pay for Asian food any more. I heard the same gripe from a beef kway teow hawker in Geylang. People will gladly pay good money for a mediocre dish of spaghetti bolognese but won't shell out for good Chinese or Peranakan food, even though the latter almost always takes way more time and effort to make. No one really appreciates how much time and effort goes into making say...a beef rendang or a bowl of laksa any more, or how many different ingredients go into it. A Peranakan

Do anybody make real shit anymore?

Future looks bleak dude...

chap chye looks deceptively easy and cheap to make. It's just a vegetable dish after all. But what you don't see is what goes into making that intense prawn and pork stock which in turn is the base for that deliciously moreish umami bomb of a gravy, or the different types of vegetables, fungi and bean curd which give the dish its vibrancy in colour, taste and texture.

All the while, in my head rings: *this is it*. The future will be a boring and bleak one populated by sterile air-conditioned food courts (food courts being the lesser cousins of hawker centres) all serving mediocre meals tasting the same and coming vacuum-sealed, pre-packed, pre-cooked and pre-prepped from some nameless factory somewhere in the boondocks. But I don't blame any of the stallholders though. At the end of the day, it is a business and a livelihood for them and they have to watch the bottom line. Buying food directly from the factory is probably the most time- and cost-efficient. It is also not helped by an age in which some people are just not as willing to spend money on good Singaporean food any more. And appreciating it for what it truly is.

As Tolstoy once said, "Everyone thinks of changing the world, but no one thinks of changing himself." And this is why we all need to learn how to cook. It's just a matter of whether one has the passion or interest to do so, and whether one can be bothered to put in the time and effort to learn how to. Some things don't even require elbow grease. Take making a stock: It literally involves dumping a whole bag of bones into a pot. And then bringing it up to a boil. That's it.

In a city where the landscape changes faster than Clark Kent's costume change in a phone booth, food is the one special thing in our heritage and culture that we have proprietary control over. And if we change our ways and learn to cook the foods we love, then absolutely nothing can bulldoze, acquire, compulsorily en bloc or redevelop that.

Unless , of course, you are one lazy sonofa...

Finding Your Own G-Spot

My friend Jeremy once told me about an incident he'd witnessed at Kenny Shopsin's eponymous New York City restaurant, Shopsins, which is notorious for its multiple rules (including, but not limited to: no copying your neighbour's order, no parties bigger than four and no ordering off-the-menu items), its infamous 900-item menu and of course, Kenny himself. A lady sat down next to Jeremy one day and was looking increasingly flustered at the sheer volume of choices on the menu. She then proceeded to do what any normal human being would do at a restaurant, and asked a waiter what he'd recommend. The restless waiter stopped fiddling with his order pad, looked

> If we change our ways and learn to cook the foods we love, then absolutely nothing can bulldoze, acquire, compulsorily en bloc or redevelop that.

down at her with a raised eyebrow and, after an awkward, pregnant silence, yelled the lady's request across the restaurant to Kenny, who was perched on a bar stool behind the counter like a grand high priest. Kenny slowly unfolded his thickset arms, which were crossed over his portly tummy, sat upright and, without a moment's hesitation, hollered back across the entire restaurant, "HEY LADY! YOU GOTTA FIND YOUR OWN G-SPOT!"

Another story: When I first moved to London on my own, I asked my mum to give me her recipe for Hainanese pork chops. I got an email that went something like this: "Use knife to tenderise pork. Add soya sauce and pepper to marinate. Dip in egg and breadcrumbs and fry." The one thing consistent in all the recipes she sent was that there were no measurements. And I am pretty sure my mum isn't alone in this regard. When I asked around, this seemed to be de rigueur for any mum, grandmother or person born pre-Internet and pre-bell bottom jeans. It was always a pinch, a splash, a handful or a drizzle.

I used to think that maybe they were just being intentionally difficult and refusing to pass on their legacies. But I realised this wasn't the case. Cooking *is* all about feeling, and all these brilliant cooks from halcyon days of yore cooked from their hearts and not from cookbooks, iPads or websites. Instinctively, they fine-tuned the taste of the dishes as they fried, tossed, whisked and stirred, adding pinches of this and splashes of that.

So why am I telling you these two stories, which awkwardly place two phrases, which should never ever be together, on the same page: 'my mum' and 'G-spot' (*cringe*)?

Well, because, simply put, I *can't* find your G-spot for you.

Some, if not, most of the recipes in this cookbook have been decoded into precise quantifiable amounts, timings and methods gathered from anecdotes, scrawls and scribblings by various mothers and grandmothers. But the recipes are merely guides to help you make what *I* like to eat. I'm pretty sure I don't have the exact same palette as you. You might like things dead salty or ultra spicy. Or prefer your vegetables crunchier, or overcooked until they resemble baby food. You might like your desserts diabetes-inducingly sweet or face-scrunchingly sour.

As you try out the recipes in this book, hopefully you too will be inspired to experiment and to *feel* your food—tasting and adjusting to your own preferences as you go along. I had no idea how to cook when I first started. Hell, I only knew how to cook tinned spaghetti. It was only through trial and error that I taught myself the dishes in this book.

So go on, be brave. Who knows? In the end, you might just find your very own G-spot.

BASICS

PREP!!!

INGREDIENTS AND METHODS

Agar

A gelatin-like substance derived from seaweed, agar is commonly found in long, dried strips or in powdered form. It was used in the making of jelly-like desserts in Southeast Asia long before the Western culinary world realised its potential, and can now be found by the truckload in achingly cool hipster restaurants serving 'molecular gastronomy' cuisine. Sometimes the powders and strips come pre-coloured too—perfect if you're making jellies for a kiddy party.

Belacan

If there is any ingredient a self-respecting Southeast Asian home cook should have, it's belacan. Made by fermenting and drying tiny shrimp under the blazing hot sun for days and then grinding and compacting it into the dense blocks you will commonly find in Asian supermarkets, it is probably the most pungent (or fragrant) monster you will have in your larder. When a teeny amount is added to your cooking, it imparts the most phenomenal rich depth of flavour to any dish, giving it an instant unparalleled umami hit. Whenever I use belacan, I like to lightly toast it before using it (see *Toasting*).

Cardamon

Small, dried, light green seed pods about the size of a raisin, cardamon tastes minty and woody with a slight hint of anise. A little goes a long way, so don't use too many at once. If you are frying these, stand back as they are likely to pop and splatter searing hot oil in your direction. Found in most Chinese and Indian supermarkets.

Chai Poh

This is dried, preserved turnip, and can usually be found in most Asian supermarkets in either a sweet or salty version. Sometimes it's sold pre-grated, which is helpful. Remember to soak chai poh before using, rinsing out the water a few times, as it can be very salty.

Chillies

Three types of chillies are used throughout this book: dried red chillies, red bird's eye chillies and conventional long red chilli peppers. They all have very different flavour profiles. Dried red chillies have a very latent slow-burn spiciness, red bird's eye chillies are the exact opposite with a punch-you-in-the-face-spiciness and the conventional red chilli peppers have a fresh, spicy zing to them.

Cincalok

Like belacan, cincalok is made by fermenting tiny shrimp with salt and rice. It is a wet pinkish gloop and is incredibly pungent, but when you add diced chillies, shallots and a squirt of lime, it can make the most sublime dipping sauce. Cincalok is often sold sealed in a glass bottle, but because it continues to ferment, the pressure builds up inside the glass bottle and unless you want to redecorate your apartment with this, I suggest you take it outside and open it *very* carefully.

Cinnamon

Cinnamon comes from the inner bark of the cinnamon tree and can be found either rolled up in cylinders or in powder form. It is readily available in supermarkets.

Cloves

Earthy, warm, herby, spicy and slightly sweet, cloves are dried-up flower buds and can be very overpowering, so use sparingly. They can be found in most supermarkets.

Coriander Powder

Pre-ground coriander powder will work well for all the recipes in this book. If you want a brighter, more intense flavour, you can buy whole coriander seeds and toast them off in a dry frying pan before grinding them into powder, like the old school and hardcore.

Eggs

I like to use eggs from happy, free-roaming chickens because they're just so much tastier and taste...well...eggier. Yolks from free-range eggs are a luminous bright orange and have an unbeatably creamy and luscious texture when poached and left runny. Battery-chicken eggs just look limp and pale in comparison. Bear in mind, however, that there is no international authority or benchmark for what constitutes 'free-range' or 'organic', leading to a fair number of scams and mis-labelling in supermarkets, so always do your research and buy from a trusted source.

Fish Sauce

Fish sauce is a dark, amber-red, thin liquid that is made by fermenting fish in large vats with salt for long periods of time. In London, I use Squid brand fish sauce as it seems to be the most readily available. Like belacan, fish sauce brings a whole dimension of umami to any dish. Use sparingly though, as fish sauce can quickly render a dish too fishy and salty. You can also experiment and use it in other cuisines where salt is

required. I have used it to make bolognese and it was bloody fantabulous.

Fried Shallots and Fried Shallot Oil

Everyone should have this magical oil in their larder. It kicks every dish up a notch just by sprinkling a dash. Finely slice shallots and shallow fry them in 5 cm of hot vegetable oil on medium heat. After about 15 minutes or when the shallots have just started to turn golden brown, remove the pan from the heat and set aside. Let cool and strain the fragrant oil. Add a sprinkle of salt and dry the fried shallots on sheets of kitchen paper. Store both separately in airtight containers and sprinkle onto salads, noodles and stir-fries.

Galangal

Also called *lengkuas* or blue ginger, galangal looks very much like common ginger, but its skin is paler in colour and it is far harder, requiring you to put in some work to chop that bad boy up. It tastes nothing like regular ginger though, and has an almost pine-like and citrusy perfume.

Gula Melaka

If any of the recipes call for gula melaka, you must try your best to hunt it down. There is

simply no substitute. It is made from the sap of the palm tree and is sometimes called 'palm sugar' in shops. It is a deep, intense dark brown in colour, often comes in cylindrical shapes (from being let to set and dry in bamboo sections) and has a rich, buttery, almost creamy taste reminiscent of smoky burnt caramel that cannot be substituted. Gula melaka from the Malaysian town of Malacca is the best.

Hae Bee

Nicknamed 'Flavours' Little Helpers' by *The New York Times*, hae bee are small sundried shrimp and most of the ones you will find in the super-markets are about the size of a thumbnail each (although you can sometimes find larger ones in Hong Kong, which are effectively the same thing). Often used in a sauce or soup base, they inject a briny seafoody flavour to any dish. Soak them in a little bit of warm water to rehydrate them before use.

Hae Gor

A very thick, gloopy, dark-as-night shrimp paste, this is not too dissimilar from belacan in that they are both made by sunning the life out of teeny shrimp. It is also bloody pungent (or fragrant).

Ikan Bilis

These dried anchovies are slightly different from the anchovies you might be used to seeing in Italian food. Although dried, they pack just as much umami flavour with less of the fishiness, and are dirt cheap in most Asian dried food stores.

Kaffir Lime Leaves

You can spot these distinctive leaves by their thick, waxy, pea-green hue and double leaf lobes. They have a distinctive citrus scent and I cannot think of any substitute for this. To use, discard the thick centre spine of each leaf, roll it up and slice it ultra finely. Sometimes you can find them in the frozen section of Chinese supermarkets.

Kecap Manis

This is a sweet soya sauce with a consistency that is almost syrupy due to the addition of sugar, resulting in a treacle-like sauce. It is mostly used as a dipping sauce.

Laksa Leaves

A bowl of laksa is simply an ordinary bowl of noodle curry without these leaves. I cannot stress how integral they are to the dish. Without them, you might as well make something else. In London, they can be pretty hard to find and often are not called laksa leaves. The sales assistant may not know what

you are yapping on about, but don't be fooled: this cunning leaf comes under various guises, including Vietnamese mint, Cambodian mint, *rau ram*, hot mint, *daun kesom* or *daun laksa*.

Lap Cheong

This is a variety of Chinese sausage not too different from Spanish chorizo, and is commonly used in Cantonese cooking. It is hard, dried and cured, and is usually made from pork and fat, although you can also find ones made from duck liver as well. They can be very hard, so make sure you have a sharp knife when cutting these.

Lemongrass

Most commonly used in Thai cooking, these long, hard stalks are actually tightly rolled leaves. They smell absolutely lovely— fresh, clean and full of citrusy goodness, like lemon zest on acid. When choosing lemongrass, look for firm, hard stalks where the bottom half is a white-ish faint yellow in colour and the tips are a lively green.

Lily Buds

Dried yellow-gold strands vaguely resembling its Cantonese namesake, *kum jum*, which means 'golden needles', these are often found in most well-stocked Chinese supermarkets in the dried

goods section near the shiitake mushrooms. They need to be pre-soaked in lukewarm water before cooking.

Lontong

This is basically a very compressed rice cake in the shape of a cylinder wrapped with a banana leaf. Often found sliced in certain curry dishes in Southeast Asian cooking as a form of carbohydrate, like an alternative to potatoes. To make your own, pack partially cooked rice into a roll, wrap with a banana leaf and compress the hell out of it so it's all mushed up and compact. Then steam till cooked.

Mentaiko

Ochre or deep red in colour, this is the marinated roe of cod or pollock, often left in their natural egg-sac membranes and sold as such. Commonly found in Japanese supermarkets.

Mui Choy

In Southeast Asia, most of the time mui choy comes all semi-dried, wrinkly and speckled generously with salt and/or sugar just lying there, uncovered in the market. In London, mui choy goes by another name —preserved mustard greens— and can be found vacuum-packed in your standard Chinatown supermarket. Like most preserved products, always remember to soak first and change the soaking water regularly, or else it will be ridiculously salty.

Noodles

The recipes in this cookbook call for all sorts of noodles. Bee hoon is a thin, white vermicelli rice noodle and requires some soaking before use as it is often found in the dried goods section. Kway teow is a flat, white rice noodle which is often found fresh in Chinese markets although you can sometimes find it dried too. Laksa noodles are a thicker version of bee hoon and have a slippery texture, almost akin to Japanese udon but thinner, and can be found in both dried and fresh versions. I would stick to whatever noodles the recipe calls for. Theoretically most of these noodles can be used interchangeably but that would be like swapping spaghetti with macaroni and trying to make macaroni bolognese.

Oil

For most of Southeast Asian cooking, oil is used as a base for stir-frying so it's overwhelmed by the flavours and smells of the spices and herbs used in the dishes. Therefore I just use a neutral vegetable, peanut, sunflower or rapeseed oil. Your cold-pressed, unfiltered olive oil from Ligurian olives

harvested by hand will be wasted in the recipes here.

Pandan Leaves

Also known as screwpine leaves in some parts of the world, these are the long, bright green, blade-like leaves of the tropical pandanus plant. They are used in plenty of Southeast Asian cuisine and as natural green food colouring in desserts. The leaves' juices and, more importantly, their fragrance—which I can only describe as a combination of jasmine, rose, hay and freshly cut grass —is extracted by blending and pounding.

Rempah

The heart and soul of many Singaporean dishes, especially curries, rempah is the basic foundation of a dish, which, depending on how well it is made, can either elevate or destroy the dish. At its most fundamental, a basic rempah is a paste made from garlic, galangal, ginger, shallots and red chillies. Some cooks then add lemongrass, coriander seeds, candlenuts and belacan, depending on what dish is being made and attuning the flavours to one's likes and dislikes.

The old-school cats will insist on using a granite mortar and pestle to diligently pound away at those rhizomes, herbs, spices, seeds and nuts.

Alternatively, you can, like me, just blitz it all in a blender, which is much quicker and easier. You want to achieve a wet paste-y consistency so as you blitz or pound away, slowly drizzle in vegetable oil until you have reached the desired consistency. Because rempah is such a hassle to make, I always make much more than required and either refrigerate or freeze it in small batches. When you want to use the rempah, heat the oil in the pan over medium-low heat, and when the oil is hot, add the raw rempah, constantly stirring to ensure it does not burn. Once it turns a deep, dark reddish-brown, becomes intensely fragrant and you see the oil slowly separating from the rempah, it's raring and ready to rock and roll.

Sago

A starch extracted from tropical palms that is often found in Asian supermarkets in the form of miniscule, hard white balls or 'pearls'. Not to be confused with the pearls used for the Taiwanese drink bubble tea (which are often made of tapioca).

Salt

None of the recipes here require you to use fancy one-million-year-old salt that has been excavated from some dried-up Jurassic period sea bed or pink Himalayan mountain salt. Unless otherwise stated, all the recipes in this book use fine sea salt. I prefer sea salt as it is less processed, but normal table salt is fine as well.

Shaoxing Rice Wine
An essential addition to any Chinese larder, this wine has been around for centuries in China and is made by fermenting brown glutinous rice, which gives it an auburn hue. It is heavily perfumed, savoury, nutty and almost akin to a dry sherry (which is sometimes suggested as a last-resort substitute).

Soaking
A fair number of dried products are used in this book, from prawns and cuttlefish to shiitake mushrooms and wood ear fungus. Though soaking times vary for each ingredient, a soak of at least 4 hours in warm water should do the trick of reconstituting the dried goods. Use your own judgement and touch it. If it's all swelled up and not hard any more, it should be good to use. Small shrimp require less time to reconstitute, but for a big, good-quality shiitake mushroom, you should soak it overnight in room-temperature water. If you are really rushing for time, soak the ingredient in a bowl of hot water for an hour, though this is not ideal as you end up cooking it at the same time as opposed to just reconstituting it.

Soya Sauce
A good premium soya sauce should not only be moderately salty but also impart a full-bodied, rounded, strong umami taste, which is produced by the lengthy natural fermentation of the soya beans—as opposed to a cheap, one-note hit of extreme saltiness. The brand I love most is Kwong Woh Hing. Not only is it a homegrown Singaporean brand but, as opposed to cheap soya sauce which is largely made from chemical MSG flavour enhancers and the addition of high levels of salt and other additives, Kwong Woh Hing still manufacture their soya sauce manually, with the same methods they have been using for the past 60 years, leaving the beans and saltwater in large antique urns to naturally ferment and brew under the scorching Singapore sun for at least one year. There are light and dark versions. The darker versions are usually less salty. There is also a thick, syrupy version, which is much less salty and often used as a dipping sauce for Hainanese chicken rice.

Star Anise
Star anise imparts a strong licouricey, aniseedy flavour to foods and should be used sparingly. Try to use whole stars as they are easier to find, and remove before eating as they're hard and tough as nails. There is a chemical compound in star anise which reacts with onions, and it enhances the flavour of meat when cooked. Found in most Chinese and Indian supermarkets.

Sugar
Unless otherwise stated, just use good ol' granulated or white sugar. There is no need for any fancy caster or icing sugar.

Tamari Soya Sauce
This differs from our traditional Chinese soya sauce in that there is little or no wheat included and it uses a far greater concentration of fermented soya beans. This results in a more aromatic, smoother, richer and more complex flavour and is also less salty than traditional soya sauce.

Tamarind Pulp
Tamarind, also known as *assam* in Malay, is extremely sour and is often sold in the form of a semi-dried, soft paste, like a block of Plasticine. To use, just soak it in some warm water and then strain to remove any seeds.

Tau Cheo

Made from fermented yellow beans that are usually mashed up into a wet paste or left whole and swimming in brine. Although either can be used interchangeably, I live by the words a stallholder once told me: "Use whole beans better".

Tau Kee

Also known as yuba, tofu skin, bean curd skin or bean curd sheet. When soya beans are crushed and boiled to make soya milk, a film or skin forms on the liquid surface. This is then dried and sold. All Asian supermarkets should have them. They come in varied sizes, from long, curled up ones to paper-thin, fragile flat ones. These are all pretty much the same and just have varying textures and cooking times.

Tau Pok

You can find these in the refrigerated section of Chinese supermarkets, most probably next to the tofu, as it comes from the same family. Tau pok is made simply by deep-frying firm tofu (bean curd), so if you can't find it, it is not that difficult to make it yourself.

Toasting

Desiccated Coconut, Peanuts, Sesame Seeds, Belacan
Remember that the whole point of toasting is to add colour, crunch, texture and above all, release fragrant oils, so the very last thing you want to do is burn whatever you're toasting. Watch the pan like a hawk. Desiccated coconut, peanuts, sesame seeds and belacan burn incredibly easily so you need to constantly toss and stir everything.

Before you toast belacan, remove all laundry or expensive fabric from the immediate vicinity and shut the kitchen doors and open all windows. I'm warning you now.

Heat a dry pan over high heat and when the pan is hot, add the coconut/peanuts/sesame seeds/belacan and toast it slowly, stirring regularly. Remove from the heat when (a) the coconut and sesame seeds turn a medium shade of pinewood brown (b) you start to smell the aroma of the peanuts (c) when the belacan turns a shade darker and your apartment starts smelling like a musky fermented fish packaging sweatshop.

Set aside immediately as everything will continue cooking in the residual heat.

Turmeric

The crazy will buy a whole fresh turmeric and dry it up till it looks like a shrivelled Chinese testicle before grinding that into powder. The rest, like myself, just buy ground turmeric from shops.

White Pepper

If you can somehow get access to Sarawak white pepper from your neighbourhood pepper smuggler, you should try to get it. If not, regular white pepper you can find in your local supermarket will do nicely. If you want to take it up a notch, you can use freshly (but still finely) ground white pepper, but you'll have to put in a bit of elbow grease to get it as fine as what you get out of a bottle. To get white pepper, the dark husk of the pepper fruit has been removed, leaving the white pepper seed. Without the harsh bold flavours of the dark husk, white pepper is far more delicate and perfumed, adding an almost musky and woody fragrance to your dishes.

You Char Kway

Also known in Mandarin as *you tiao*, these long, deep-fried pieces of savoury dough are similar to doughnuts. But in addition to eating them on their own, we use them in all sorts of other things—from slicing them up and adding them to congee, to adding them to sweet desserts like tau suan or simply dunking them in soya milk. We also use them in rojak, a fruit salad of sorts.

LARD

Liquid Gold

Most, if not all, of the dishes in this book are homages to Fat and his savoury sidekick Salt. Although Fat has had a pretty rubbish reputation in Singapore since my teenage years, what with the repeated government campaigns, slogans and posters telling all and sundry about the evils of sodium and fatty foods, my mum and generations of grannies and Peranakan aunties have held their ground like true rebels and insisted on cooking their chicken rice with rendered chicken fat and frying vegetables with lard, like the Che Guevaras of the Deliciousness Movement. If anyone were to tell you otherwise, well, here's what my mum has to say: "Look at your granny, she lived 'til about a gabazillion years old, had a headful of black hair 'til the end and was all lucid and chirpy. Do you really think that was thanks to a diet of poly-unsaturated fats, macrobiotic pills and a sodiumless diet? Of course not lah!"

While any vegetable oil is a fair substitute for lard and all the recipes herein state vegetable oil for convenience, if you want to lift your meal from being the equivalent of a family saloon car into a hyper-speed, pimped-up, Jetsons-style supercar, use lard with haste.

How to Render Lard

An immediate by-product of rendering lard is that your house will smell incredibly porky, so if you have any pork haters or vegetarians as housemates, warn them in advance or just don't do it in their kitchen.

Firstly, get your hands on some pork fat. You'll end up with an almost one-to-one fat to rendered lard ratio so go by that measurement when deciding how much pork fat you'll need. Lard freezes very well so you should always make more than you need.

Ask your local butcher nicely for some pork fat trimmings. Get your butcher to remove any meat or skin there may be on the fat, because it is a real bitch of an effort to do this yourself at home unless you have the knife skills of a trained assassin. You might want to push your luck and ask him to mince up the fat as this increases the surface area and therefore greatly helps in the rendering process. If not,

just chop it up into small 2.5-cm cubes yourself.

Secondly, place the cubed or minced pork fat into a deep, heavy cast-iron casserole pot (the heat is more evenly distributed in one of these bad boys). Add water to a depth of 1 cm. Chuck the pot into the oven at 180°C for at least 2 hours, checking and stirring it every half hour. It's done when you get a decent amount of lard in the pot and the non-renderable bits in the lard are slowly turning brown and either floating around or sticking to the bottom of the pot.

Remove from the oven and using extreme care, pour the blazing hot fat through a metal strainer. The crispy crackling left in the strainer is a magical ingredient that can be sprinkled on just about anything for maximum piggyness. It can be refried again to make it extra crispy but be careful not to burn it.

After the lard has cooled slightly, transfer to mason jars. Use immediately or let cool and store in the freezer. It will keep for up to 3 months.

OH MY LARD

STOCK OF AGES

The Stock That Takes Ages, Keeps for Ages and Rocks All Ages

The key behind some of the dishes in this book is a simple, good, milky, rich stock, and in order to achieve that, you definitely do not peel open a stock cube or buy supermarket premade stock. Make sure you get good-quality carcasses and bones from your butcher. If the bones are too big, ask your butcher nicely to saw it into pot-sized portions for you. And be ready to boil those bones hard! Bones contain marrow which, when boiled over extended periods of time, will release proteins and contribute to the rich intensity and depth of flavour that you really want. The cartilage and the ligaments at the ends of the bones provide the collagen which then help thicken the stock and give it its creamy texture. This collagen also helps it congeal into a wobbly jelly. A jelly of awesome.

MAKES 3–4 LITRES

8 chicken carcasses
1.5 kg pork bones
500 g dried shrimp (hae bee)
100 g ikan bilis (dried anchovies) (optional)
Sea salt

Throw all the chicken carcasses and pork bones into the biggest pot you can find. Pour boiling water over everything, then drain. This removes any dirt from the bones. Refill the pot with enough room-temperature water to cover all the bones. Add the dried shrimp and ikan bilis and let it slowly come to a rolling boil.

Skim the scum off the surface and constantly top up the water. Let it boil for a minimum of 8 hours, or as long as you desire. (I once boiled stock for over 3 days, letting it simmer overnight in the stockpot when I was asleep.)

You should aim to attain a thick, creamy-coloured stock with a consistency not unlike that of full-cream milk. Remove the bones and reserve. You can season the stock at this stage and use it straightaway, but if you wish to intensify the flavour, continue reducing it until you have reached the desired intensity. Alternatively, reduce the stock to a fifth of its original volume and let cool, then freeze in individual ice cube trays, ready to use when you need to add a blast of flavour to your dishes. The stock should keep for about 3 months.

Chicken Stock

Follow the recipe for Stock of Ages, but replace the pork bones with the equivalent weight of chicken carcasses and halve the boiling time. To thin the stock, just add more water.

Meat Shreds

Because I do not like to waste food, I like to take the reserved bones from the stock, let them cool, and then peel and scrape all the meat off the bones with clean hands (it's easier than using a fork). This shredded meat can be added to dishes such as chap chye, laksa, or just about anything saucey. You can also freeze the meat shreds for later use. There may not be as much flavour any more thanks to the overzealous boiling, but they still provide good, meaty bite and texture, absorbing and carrying the flavour of the sauce or stock.

RICE
A Boring Bowl of Rice

SHU HAN: There is just something so essential and comforting about a 'boring' bowl of rice accompanying an Asian meal. But you'll be surprised how many people can't get it right. It was the hardest thing for me to make when I first started to cook for myself. It either clumps, or isn't cooked on the inside, or is both of them at the same time. I have two favourite varieties of long grain rice: basmati rice to go with curries or for fried rice, and jasmine rice to go with most other Singaporean food. The methods are a bit different because you want slightly different end results.

Rinse

So many people don't seem to find this step important, but it is. They say it used to be necessary to remove talc in old processing methods, but rinsing does more than that. You remove surface starch, prevent the rice from clumping later, and rinsing just makes the rice cleaner overall and fresher tasting. Put the uncooked rice in plenty of water and swirl and swish and massage.

Wash till the water runs almost clear, though it won't ever be totally clear.

Soak (Only for Basmati)

Soaking makes the basmati rice grains really long and slender. Ideally, I try to soak it for 30 minutes. After soaking, drain the starchy water. Cooking in fresh water makes the rice grains really fluffy and separate.

Water to Rice Ratio

My mum uses this traditional method I'm sure you've all heard of: sticking your finger in and adding enough water to come to the first knuckle of the index finger. It works for her, and it works for me sometimes, if I'm doing it in a pot of the same size, and for about the same amount of rice. But I don't know if it will work for a big guy with giant fingers. The more conventional ratio I always hear about is 2:1. I don't know how it can work for people because I always get mush with 2:1.

For jasmine rice, I use a water to rice ratio of 1¼:1.

For basmati rice, I do 1:1, slightly more if it isn't soaked.

What Else?

If using basmati rice, add a drop or two of ghee or some other oil to your rice cooker or saucepan, depending on which method you choose.

Most Western cooks also seem to advocate salting the rice. I guess it's all good and fine if you want to, but most Asian cooks don't.

The Rice-cooker Way

1. Add water and rice to the cooker. (And oil if using basmati rice.) Cook according to manufacturer's instructions.
2. Do the 'close and wait, open and fluff, close and wait, open and breathe'. When it's done, do not open the lid for 10 minutes. Then open and fluff with a chopstick or fork but not a spoon. Close and let steam for another 5 minutes. Open for a minute or so to let excess moisture evaporate, and take the time to breathe in the wonderful fragrance. You can eat it at this stage or keep it warm for a while longer till you want to eat.

The Stovetop Way

1. Add the water and rice to a saucepan. (And oil if using **+**

+ basmati rice.) Bring to a boil over medium-high heat.
2. Once it starts boiling, turn the heat down to medium and let it simmer for about 15 minutes, a bit less if it's soaked basmati rice. Or just until you see most of the water has been absorbed and you see craters.
3. Turn the heat down to very low, and cook for another 10 minutes.
4. Remove from the heat, and do the 'close and wait, open and fluff, close and wait, open and breathe'.

So What Is Perfect Rice?

For basmati, it's that unique basmati aroma, and the fluffy, long separate grains of rice. Not sticky, not dry either, but loose enough for the rice to flow easily when you run your spoon (or hands) through it.

For jasmine rice, it's that warm jasmine scent. The grains should be soft but not mushy, and plumper than basmati rice. Not sushi-rice-sticky enough to pick up in a clump with a pair of chopsticks, but less dry than basmati, so you can shovel it safely from bowl to mouth with your chopsticks (bowl being just in front of your mouth, of course).

STARTERS

Achar 52
Rojak 54
Bak kut teh 58
Chwee kueh 60
Fried Carrot Cake 62
Roti John 64
+ Tomato-chilli sauce 65
Cocktail Sausage Buns 68
Bak kwa 70
Sardine Puffs 74
Otak otak 76
Lemongrass Pork Skewers 80
Chinese Pork Belly Satay 86
Jiu Hu Char 88
Popiah 92
Kueh Pie Tee 93
Ngoh Hiang 96
Spiced Blood Cake and Fermented Pear 100

TODAY'S MENU!

I once told someone that "achar is a Singaporean take on an Indian pickle" and I guess that sums it up pretty well. Achar is a brilliant example of the meeting of two different food cultures, just like kari ayam and beef rendang. We like to serve it at the supper club as a pre-starter with crackers, and let the spicy, piquant and sweet flavours get everyone's tastebuds excited for the meal ahead. Giving a recipe for achar is a bit like giving a recipe for a simple salad: everyone has their own likes and dislikes. So be creative and improvise, find your own G-spot, use the same rempah (spice paste) but substitute with whatever vegetables you like (hard, crunchy vegetables usually work better) and whatever is in season.

ACHAR

Spicy Peranakan Vegetable Pickles

MAKES ABOUT 4 JARS

1 medium cucumber, deseeded and cut into thin, matchstick-length batons

2 medium carrots, cut into thin, matchstick-length batons

5 tbsp coarse sea salt

Half a white cabbage, cut into thin, matchstick-length strips

15 long beans, cut into matchstick-length pieces

1 pineapple, cut into bite-sized pieces

2 tbsp vegetable oil

100 g white sesame seeds, plus additional for garnishing; toasted (see page 43)

100 g raw peanuts, plus additional for garnishing; toasted (see page 43) and crushed

200 ml rice wine vinegar

2 tbsp fish sauce

Zest and juice from 4 limes

6 tbsp sugar

REMPAH (SPICE PASTE)

10 shallots

6 cloves garlic

12 fresh red chillies

2 candlenuts or macadamia nuts

1 (2.5-cm) piece galangal

2 tbsp belacan (dried shrimp paste), toasted (see page 43)

2 tsp ground turmeric

Toss the cucumber and carrots evenly in a bowl with the coarse sea salt. Let sit in the fridge, uncovered, for an hour, to extract as much moisture as possible. Rinse and drain. Dry the cucumber and carrots, cabbage, long beans and pineapple with a tea towel as much as possible—the drier, the better. Some people dry them in the sun or in a warm oven, but I really am not that fussed.

Blend all the ingredients for the rempah in a food processor or pound with a mortar and pestle until a smooth paste is formed. Heat the oil in a wok and fry the rempah over medium heat. The rempah will start off watery, but be patient and slowly fry it as you want the paste to be dry and the flavours to intensify. Turn off the heat when the oil separates and the rempah becomes intensely fragrant, about 30 minutes.

Add the cucumber and carrots, cabbage, long beans and pineapple to the wok and ensure everything is evenly coated with the rempah. Stir over low heat for about 5 minutes and then remove the wok from the heat.

Gently mix the fried vegetables, sesame seeds, peanuts, rice wine vinegar, fish sauce, lime zest, lime juice and sugar in a bowl. Season with salt to taste. If you prefer your achar more face-scrunchingly sour, add more lime juice and vinegar. If you prefer yours more sweet, add more sugar.

To store, pour into sterilised glass jars, ensuring that the vegetables are fully submerged in pickle juice. Let sit in the fridge overnight for all the sweet, spicy and sour flavours to intimately commingle. Sprinkle on more sesame seeds and peanuts before serving. Achar will keep, refrigerated, for about 10 days.

JASON: Rojak is unlike any salad you'll get in the Western world and is possibly one of the only 'salads' that Singaporean cuisine has in its repertoire. I love that one of the principal ingredients is deep-fried you char kway, which are essentially Chinese doughnuts, definitely not something you would find in one of those healthy rabbit-food salads of the Western world. The combination of tangy, sweet pineapple, crunchy bangkwang (yam bean), fresh cucumber chunks and crispy you char kway creates the most lovely medley of textures and flavours. The magical dressing uses an unusual black shrimp paste, known as 'hae gor' in Singapore or *petis udang* in Malay, and not to be confused with dried shrimp paste (belacan). This sweet, molasses-like, sticky gunge gives rojak its distinctive, pungent aroma and richness, and is packed with so much umami, you could eat it off a spoon. Expect to become territorial and engage violently with anyone who fights you for the leftovers.

ROJAK

A Fruit and Vegetable Salad. With Fried Doughnuts.

FEEDS 4–6

DRESSING

1–2 tsp chilli paste

2 tbsp gula melaka (palm sugar)

1 tbsp belacan (dried shrimp paste),
 toasted (see page 43)

3 tbsp hae gor (black shrimp paste)

½ tbsp tamarind pulp

2 tbsp kecap manis (sweet soya sauce)

1 pineapple, coarsely chopped into
 2-cm chunks

1 small bangkwang (yam bean),
 peeled and coarsely chopped into
 2-cm chunks

Half a cucumber, halved lengthwise
 and coarsely chopped into
 2-cm chunks

100 g bean sprouts, tailed and
 lightly blanched

200 g raw peanuts, toasted (see page 43),
 skinned and coarsely chopped

1 stick you char kway (fried doughstick),
 briefly toasted in a hot oven and
 cut into 2-cm pieces

To make the dressing, blend the chilli paste, gula melaka and belacan in a food processor or pound with a mortar and pestle until a smooth paste is formed. Add the hae gor, tamarind pulp and kecap manis. Mix until well-combined and set aside.

Just before serving, mix the pineapple, bangkwang, cucumber and bean sprouts (or other fruits and vegetables of your choosing) in a large bowl. Add the dressing and the peanuts (reserving some for garnishing) and mix well.

To serve, spoon into small bowls and garnish with reserved peanuts. Rojak is traditionally eaten with bamboo skewers (and remarkable dexterity and psychomotor skills). Serve accordingly and snigger as your guests inevitably fumble.

TIP: Omit the bangkwang (yam bean) if you can't find it. Any combination of crunchy fruits and vegetables, such as unripe mango, green apple and papaya, or blanched kangkong (morning glory) will work just as well too.

THE
GREAT

BKT
CHALLENGE

Literally translated as the utterly unappetising 'meat bone tea', bak kut teh is made by simmering pork bones with herbs and spices for hours or days on end and is often served with steamed rice and you char kway (fried doughsticks). No other dish in the history of Singapore and Malaysia's culinary rivalry rallies citizens into flag-waving patriots as much as this one. The Singaporean version is conventionally a clear, peppery broth, while the Malaysian version is a dark, herbal broth—but both are fiercely defended to the death by their respective countrymen.

In the summer of 2012, Jason very innocently tweeted about how awesome he thought his Singaporean bak kut teh dinner had been. This snowballed into a heated, all-out debate littered with trash talk between us and a bunch of Malaysians, led by Yolanda Augustin of Wild Serai supper club. To settle this once and for all, a date was set for the grudge match to end all grudge matches. The Great Bak Kut Teh Challenge was staged under the guise of raising money for our pet charity, Action Against Hunger, but each of us knew that there was way more at stake. Punters had to vote for their favourite version and, if they wanted to, make donations to Action Against Hunger according to the one they preferred.

The result? Well, I am thoroughly pleased to say that after all that bubble-bubble-toil-and-trouble that went into my cauldron of bak kut teh, Singapore not only raised the most money, but won the People's Choice Award as well! If some government official is reading this, *ahem* I would not say no to a mention at the next National Day Rally.

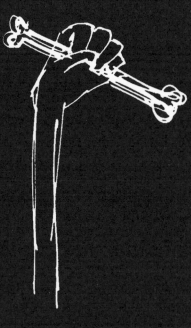

So what was my secret? Well, the version I've been cooking all these years isn't really the true-blue Singaporean version (gasp!), nor is it the Malaysian version either. It's very rich, fiercely peppery and garlicky, but at the same time subtly herbal and very dark. The key ingredient is serious shedloads of garlic. Enough, say, to make Dracula or your date wince at the sheer thought—which also means, this is probably not date food.

I am almost embarrassed to include a recipe for bak kut teh as it is so simple. If you use pre-packaged herb mixes, which are readily found in any Chinese supermarkets selling Southeast Asian ingredients, the recipe basically involves boiling the stock for an inordinately long time. You just need to make sure the stock does not dry up. That's it. Remember the story about finding your own G-spot where I encourage experimentation? This dish is probably the best place to start. The long boiling process is an open invitation for you to taste and tweak the stock. Use the recipe as a guide and then freestyle it as you go along.

BAK KUT TEH

Our Riff on the Classic Herbal Pork Rib Broth

FEEDS 6–8

JASON'S HERB MIX

2 tbsp white peppercorns

2 tbsp fennel seeds

4 star anise

12 whole cloves

2 sticks cinnamon

8 pieces dang shen
(Chilean bellflower root)

12 pieces dang gui (Chinese angelica)

20 pieces yu zhu
(Solomon's seal rhizome)

25 gou qi zi (goji berry)

1.5 kg pork spare ribs

3.3 litres water, plus additional
for blanching

1 kg large pork bones

8 heads of garlic, no need to skin

4 heaped tbsp white peppercorns
(preferably Sarawak peppercorns)

5 tbsp light soya sauce

5 tbsp dark soya sauce

Ground white pepper (optional)

Handful of fresh coriander leaves
(cilantro), to garnish

You char kway (fried doughsticks),
to serve

Dried red chillies, soaked in
lukewarm water for 1 hour and
thinly sliced, to serve

Thick dark soya sauce, to serve

To assemble the herb mix, place all the herbs and spices in a large infuser ball, or gather inside a muslin cloth and tie the ends with a string to secure. Set aside. Roughly crush the white peppercorns with the flat of a heavy cleaver or with a mortar and pestle. Place in another large infuser ball or muslin cloth with the ends tied. This prevents the bits of peppercorn from floating about so your guests won't accidentally bite into them.

To make the broth, wash the pork ribs and dump them into a large colander. Pour a large kettle of boiling water over the ribs, blanching them lightly. Bring 3.3 litres of water to a boil in your largest stockpot over high heat. When it has reached a rolling boil, chuck in the pork bones, garlic, white peppercorns, light and dark soya sauce, and herb mix. Boil hard for an hour, skimming any foamy gunk that collects on the surface. After an hour, add the pork ribs and continue boiling.

Now comes the long and arduous wait, because a good, rich stock comes to those who wait. I keep it on a rolling boil for about 3 hours before turning the heat down to low and leaving it to gently simmer overnight. Replenish the stock with water as necessary so the pork ribs and bones are always covered.

Turn off the heat and remove all the garlic heads from the stock. Squeeze whatever mush is left in the garlic skins into the stock, which should now resemble a very rich broth. Season with more light and dark soya sauce according to taste. You can also add more ground white pepper if you want it more peppery.

To serve, garnish with coriander leaves. Cut some sticks of you char kway into 2.5-cm pieces, and serve with sliced red chillies drizzled with thick dark soya sauce for dipping.

TIPS: Add dried or fresh shiitake mushrooms and tau pok (a type of bean curd) to the stock if you want more stuff to nibble on. They absorb the broth very well and explode with flavour when bitten into. Twenty minutes before serving, chuck them into the broth, turn up the heat and let it come to a rolling boil. Remove from the heat after 20 minutes.

Pre-packaged herb mixes are perfectly acceptable. Try to find those which are not pre-ground and don't contain MSG. To determine how many packets you'll need, follow the instructions on the packet but double the packet-to-water ratio stated, adjusting for the 3.3 litres of water required here.

Every time I serve chwee kueh, there's always someone who screws up their face and goes, "Eww! Preserved turnip?! On what? A gooey rice cake?!" But their look of disgust turns to euphoria and surprise when they bite into the pillowy soft, semi-translucent rice cakes and crunch on the preserved turnip (chai poh), getting a savoury, oily hit and a whiff of subtle garlickiness. Chwee kueh is an awesome starter and very easy to make. I think of it as a way to rev everyone's taste buds up a notch and set the tempo for the evening's menu. I also like to serve it the way hawkers do in Singapore: on crummy brown paper to soak up all the oil and with little toothpicks that are completely ergonomically inappropriate for the task. If you can't be bothered to make the rice cakes, you can eat the topping with bread, rice or your choice of carbs.

CHWEE KUEH

Steamed Rice Cakes with a Lardy Preserved Turnip Topping

**MAKES 25 CAKES
WITH A TRADITIONAL MOULD**

RICE CAKES

250 g rice flour

60 g tapioca flour

510 ml water, room temperature

2 tbsp vegetable oil

2 tsp fine sea salt

510 ml water, boiling

TOPPING

200 g preserved turnip (chai poh),
  soaked in warm water for 10 minutes
  and finely chopped

300 g lard (page 44) or vegetable oil

1 tbsp sesame oil

1 head garlic, finely chopped

10 dried red chillies, soaked in lukewarm
  water for 1 hour and finely chopped

3 tsp white sesame seeds

2 tsp light soya sauce

2 tsp dark soya sauce

2 tsp fish sauce

1 tbsp light brown sugar

1 tbsp sambal tumis belacan (page 118)

1 tsp Sriracha chilli sauce

2 tbsp Maggi or Lingham's sweet
  chilli sauce

To make the rice cakes, mix the rice flour, tapioca flour, room-temperature water, vegetable oil and salt in a bowl, stirring well to ensure there are no lumpy bits. Use a sieve to strain any lumps if necessary.

Transfer the mixture to a pot. Add the boiling water and simmer over low heat, stirring constantly. The mixture will thicken very quickly so don't take your eyes off it. You want to achieve the consistency of thick runny honey, a wet gluey paste or smooth oat porridge. If you think it's getting too thick and gloopy, err on the side of caution and remove the pot from the heat immediately.

To steam the rice cakes, heat your steamer with the moulds inside to warm them up. Spoon the mixture into the moulds and steam for 15–20 minutes. A skewer inserted into the rice cakes should come out clean. Remove the moulds from the steamer and leave the rice cakes to cool inside the moulds. They will keep, covered and refrigerated, for a day or two.

To make the topping, melt the lard in a heavy saucepan over high heat and add the sesame oil. Once the lard is hot, add the garlic and chillies, and fry until fragrant. Add the preserved turnip and fry for 15 minutes over low heat. Once it's super fragrant, add the sesame seeds, light soya sauce, dark soya sauce, fish sauce, sugar, sambal tumis belacan, Sriracha chilli sauce and sweet chilli sauce. Stir for another 5 minutes and remove the saucepan from the heat. Season according to taste.

To serve, remove the rice cakes from the moulds. If they are cold, re-steam or microwave them until they are spanking hot and springy again. Slap the topping generously onto the rice cakes and, if you need more kick, serve with sambal tumis belacan.

TIP: Instead of a chwee kueh mould, you can use a small sauce bowl, ramekin or any small tartlet or muffin moulds. Or you could steam the rice mixture in one big shallow bowl, making one huge rice cake which you could then slice up and serve. (Or serve it whole with a huge single dollop of turnip topping to great comic effect.)

pretty darn sexy turnip topping

pillowy soft rice cakes

SHU HAN: In the world I grew up in, carrot cake does not come with cream cheese frosting. It's hardly a cake in the dessert sense of the word, and it's not even got carrots in it, but this is carrot cake to me. A messily slapped-together plate of radish cakes scrambled with eggs and salted, preserved turnip, the best ones are fried in a generous amount of old-school, healthy lard and smeared with a spicy sambal. These homemade radish cakes are soft, but not mushily so, and are sandwiched between fluffy layers of fragrant, fish sauce-spiked egg, with just enough fried surfaces and crisp edges to keep things interesting. I like to split this into a two-stage process, making the radish cakes the day before, and cutting and frying the day after. I also tend to make more radish cakes and freeze them to easily satisfy future cravings.

FRIED CARROT CAKE

FEEDS 2–4

RADISH CAKES

100 g rice flour, sifted

150 ml water, room temperature

200 g Japanese white radish (daikon), finely grated

150 ml water, boiling

¼ tsp fine sea salt

6 tbsp lard (page 44) or vegetable oil

6 cloves garlic

75 g preserved turnip (chai poh), soaked in warm water for 10 minutes and drained

2–4 tbsp fish sauce

4 eggs

Sambal tumis belacan (page 118), to serve

Few stalks spring onions, chopped, to garnish

To make the radish cakes, mix the rice flour and room-temperature water in a metal bowl. Place the radish in a separate bowl, and pour the boiling water over it, blanching it lightly. Add the boiling water and blanched radish to the rice flour mixture. Add the salt. Set the metal bowl over a pot of boiling water, stirring the mixture until it starts to thicken into a smooth, sticky paste.

Grease a shallow dish with vegetable oil. Pour the paste into the dish and steam over medium-high heat for about 20 minutes, or until cooked and almost firm. Keep in mind that the radish cake will firm up as it cools. When the radish cake has fully cooled, cut it into small cubes. Don't worry about ragged edges as these are the bits that get irresistibly crispy during frying. Set aside.

Melt 3 tablespoons of the lard in a frying pan over high heat. When the lard is hot, add the radish cakes and fry until crispy around the edges. I like to press on them with my spatula for maximum crispiness. Once the radish cakes have browned and are just about to be charred, remove and set aside.

Add the remaining lard to the frying pan. When hot, fry the garlic and preserved turnip on high heat until fragrant. Return the radish cakes to the pan and add 1–2 tablespoons of fish sauce. Spread the ingredients evenly around the pan. Beat the eggs with the remaining 1–2 tablespoons of fish sauce and pour the beaten egg mixture evenly over the radish cakes. Let set until the bottom is nicely browned, before flipping over and browning on the other side. Roughly chop the radish cakes into smaller pieces with the sharp edge of your spatula.

To serve, smear sambal tumis belacan over the radish cakes. You can also fry the cakes directly with the sambal—that's how my favourite hawker does it. Garnish with spring onions.

BONUS: If you prefer a different, sweeter version, try the 'black' version! Instead of fish sauce, add thick dark black sauce or kecap manis and don't wait for the eggs to set before scrambling.

There was a period when I was getting a little bored with the dishes we had been serving at the supper club and wanted to shake things up a little. So the idea of a supper club evening with the theme 'No More Mr Rice Guy' was born and, yes, you guessed it, Sherlock, no rice was served. This snack was one of the first to be suggested during the brainstorming session. Essentially a baguette topped with an eggy minced lamb laced with a sweet, piquant tomato-chilli sauce, roti john was a no-brainer addition to the evening's menu.

Roti means 'bread' in Malay, while 'John' was a common nickname for Caucasian males in Singapore back in the day. Local legend has it that during the British Occupation of Singapore, when baguettes were produced for the British and introduced to Singaporeans, a young, enterprising hawker decided it would be a good idea to take the British egg baguette sandwich and mix it up a little by slathering a sinfully delicious mix of egg, minced lamb and curry spices on a side of baguette, before frying that filthy bad boy on a ghee-greased griddle and then hawking the resultant snack of sin to members of the British Empire as they took breaks from essential acts of colonisation like moustache twiddling, opium trading, cricket playing and of course, tea drinking. This hawker, completely ahead of his time, probably didn't realise that he had just invented fusion cuisine.

ROTI JOHN

Lamb and Egg Sandwich-Pizza. On Crack.

FEEDS 4

250 g minced lamb or corned beef

1 medium onion, finely chopped

2 cloves garlic, finely chopped

Small handful of fresh coriander leaves (cilantro), coarsely chopped

½ tsp ground cloves

½ tsp ground nutmeg

½ tsp ground cinnamon

Fine sea salt

Freshly ground black pepper

4 medium eggs, plus 1 additional

1 baguette, cut crosswise and then lengthwise into 4 pieces

6 tbsp vegetable oil or ghee

1 medium tomato, sliced, to garnish

Half a cucumber, sliced diagonally, to garnish

Small handful of fresh coriander leaves (cilantro), to garnish

Tomato-chilli sauce (page 65), to serve

To make the topping, mix the lamb, onion, garlic, coriander leaves, cloves, nutmeg, cinnamon, salt and pepper in a large bowl. Crack 4 eggs into the bowl and mix until well-combined. The mixture should have a runny, sloppy consistency. Let sit to marinate for at least an hour. Meanwhile, press the baguette, cut side down, onto a clean work surface to flatten it slightly, then use a spoon to make a large, shallow indentation on the cut side of the baguette.

To assemble, beat the remaining egg in a bowl. Brush the cut side of the baguette slices with the beaten egg. Spoon a layer of lamb mixture onto the cut side of the baguette, pressing down with the back of a spoon so that the lamb mixture stays in the cavity. Repeat with the rest of the baguette pieces until the lamb mixture is used up.

To cook, heat the oil or ghee (if you are feeling particularly naughty) in a large frying pan over medium-low heat. Place the baguette slices on the frying pan, meat-side down, and fry for 3 minutes, or until the meat mixture becomes fragrant and golden brown. Flip the baguette slices over and fry on the other side until the bread becomes crispy, about 2 minutes.

To serve, garnish with slices of tomato and cucumber, and fresh coriander. Serve hot with tomato-chilli sauce and, if you want, a runny sunny-side up as well if you like it even more eggy!

Shu Han is a staunch locavore who believes in eating with the seasons. In summer in London, to make tomatoes last longer, she makes a chilli-ketchup mix which, according to her, "is real, proper ketchup, rich with the sweet-tart intensity of slow-cooked tomatoes, with a punch from the spices and a little bit of old-school kick from the chilli. And of course with none of the sodium benzoate/ modified starches/ emulsifiers ending with a string of numbers." This sauce, together with roti john, is like the perfect rock-and-roll marriage: dirrrrty, messy and a whole lot of sexy.

TOMATO-CHILLI SAUCE

Never Use Heinz Again

MAKES 1 JAR

6 large tomatoes, coarsely chopped

1 large onion, finely chopped

2 cloves garlic, finely chopped

2 fresh red chillies, finely chopped (adjust according to your tolerance level)

2 star anise

5 whole cloves

1 tsp ground mustard

¼ cup molasses

¼ cup unrefined cane sugar

¼ cup apple cider vinegar

1 tbsp fine sea salt

Simmer all the ingredients in a pot over low heat for about 3–4 hours, or until the mixture becomes very thick. Let cool, then strain, discarding the cloves and the star anise. Puree in a blender and pour into a sterilised glass jar or your old squeezy bottle of Heinz (or if you're Singaporean, Maggi tomato ketchup, the relative substandard contents of which you can now throw out). The sauce will keep in the fridge for about a week or two—if it even lasts that long.

LIZZIE

Lizzie's Twitter handle (@hollowlegs) currently reads, "Food. Drink. Swears. South East London. That kind of thing". I'm not sure I can find a more apt description of this little sweetheart. In the winter of 2010, I went to my first supper club and found myself sitting next to Lizzie, a living oxymoron. Your eyes see a petite, demure, pretty half-Chinese girl but your ears hear the most foul-mouthed banter. She was free-styling and inventing swear words I'd never even heard of. And that was before she even started drinking.

Lizzie is also hopelessly influential in the foodie scene in London. With over 15,000 unique visitors a month visiting her blog, she has been namechecked by *The Guardian*'s famously anonymous restaurant critic, Marina O'Loughlin, featured in *The Sunday Times*, and has won an award from the UK's premiere lifestyle magazine *Red* for her food-blogging prowess.

LIZZIE: Hello, I'm Lizzie. I grew up in a half-Chinese, half-English household, and scones and biscuits never did much for me. I think it was the lack of pork. Instead, sausage buns, char siew puffs and curry puffs were my thing. I shunned chocolate and cream for mochi-wrapped ice cream and ice lollies made from green or red beans. Forget creamy, traditional English desserts; I was all about tropical fruits and grass jelly.

I first met Goz at a supper club—one of those places where you go and have dinner at a stranger's house and hope you make it home with both your kidneys. This was in 2010, when supper clubs, at least in London, were relatively rare. My mother would have been aghast if I'd told her I was going to some strange man's house.

I sat down nervously at the table and Goz and his three friends engulfed me with their enthusiastic chatter. It was hard to get a word in edgeways and for that I was relieved; there's not much worse than a boring dinner neighbour. The rest, they say, is history. (That "strange man" at whose house I dined is now the head chef at Momofuku Seiōbo in Sydney.)

LIZZIE: When Goz asked me to contribute a recipe for my childhood favourite, sausage buns were the first thing I thought of. They're the ideal snack: kind of dirty (you MUST NOT use posh sausages), a little sweet, and not heavy enough to ruin your dinner. Basically, perfection.

COCKTAIL SAUSAGE BUNS

Proper Old-Skool Sausage Buns You Find in a Neighbourhood Chinese Bakery

MAKES 8

350 g strong white bread flour

7 g dry yeast

100 g caster sugar

1 tsp fine sea salt

40 g salted butter, room temperature

2 eggs

160 g whole milk

8 sausages (The kind you get in brine, in a jar. No fancy ones, please.)

3 tbsp white sesame seeds

To make the dough, mix the flour, yeast, sugar, salt and butter in a large bowl. In a separate bowl, beat one of the eggs with the milk, then add to the flour mixture and stir well until everything comes together.

Dust your hands and a clean work surface with a little flour. Knead the dough for 10 minutes, or until smooth and silky, dusting with more flour if the dough becomes too sticky. (It's a little tiring, this.) Roll the dough into a ball.

Lightly grease a clean bowl and place the dough inside. Cover the bowl with clingfilm and let sit in a warm place for an hour and a half, or until the dough has doubled in size.

To assemble, divide the dough into 8 equal pieces. Roll each piece into a cylinder twice the length of each sausage, making them a little thicker in the middle. Grease a baking sheet. Place the sausages, evenly spaced, on the baking sheet and coil the dough around each of the sausages. Cover loosely with clingfilm and let sit to prove for another hour.

Preheat the oven to 190°C. Beat the remaining egg and brush on each of the proved buns. Sprinkle each bun liberally with sesame seeds. Bake for 10 minutes, or until nicely browned. Let cool on a wire rack.

If you were planning to visit Singapore and asked any expat Singaporean what she wanted from home, there's a pretty good chance she would ask for bak kwa. For all your convenient snacking needs, bak kwa is also sold vacuum-sealed in tiny, bite-sized packs, bearing an uncanny resemblance to—according to the astute observational skills of an English colleague of mine—meat condoms. Often eaten during Chinese New Year, the easiest way to describe bak kwa is that it's a sweet, savoury, sticky, smoky meat jerky. Moreish and probably not the best thing to have within reaching distance if you are on a diet.

BAK KWA

Sweet Salty Moreish Barbecued Meat Jerkies

MAKES 1 (45 BY 30-CM) BAKING SHEET

650 g pork belly, minced

100 g runny honey

150 g light brown sugar

3 tbsp Shaoxing rice wine

3 tbsp fish sauce

1 tsp sesame oil

1 tsp light soya sauce

1 tsp dark soya sauce

1 tsp five-spice powder

Few drops red food colouring (optional)

Mix all the ingredients in a large bowl until well-combined. Once the mixture resembles a firm dough, whip it viciously, picking it up with both hands and slamming it back into the bowl repeatedly (imagine your boss, ex-girlfriend, mother-in-law, that bully at school—whatever it takes) until it becomes a gooey and gluey paste. This may take anywhere between 5–15 minutes depending on the level of brute force berserking exerted on the meat clump.

To dry the meat paste, lightly grease a baking sheet or large baking tin with vegetable oil. Spread the meat paste thinly (about 3 mm) onto the baking sheet or tin. I use the back of a spoon to flatten it. Let sit in the fridge, uncovered, overnight to marinate and dry out.

The next day, if you are lucky enough to live in a hot country, you can leave the baking sheet in the sun to dry out the meat further. If, however, you are stuck in some forsaken part of the world which never sees the sun (*cough*London*cough*), invert the sheet of meat paste onto a wire rack and put it in a preheated oven at 100°C for 20 minutes with the oven door slightly ajar. Cut into desired shapes.

To serve, grill over hot charcoal for a good smoky flavour and nice char marks. Alternatively, grill in the oven at 200°C or at your oven's standard grill setting for 10 minutes or until slightly charred. Bak kwa will keep, frozen, for up to 3 months.

PHOEBE

Phoebe, an accidental member of the plusixfive family, started off posing as an incredibly caring and generous human being who volunteered to help as front of house. Her devious scheme soon fell apart when we realised that all she wanted to do was eat and take home tonnes of leftovers. One day, she piped up that she wanted to contribute a dish to the supper club. Up until that point we were only keenly aware of her skills in serving food and charming the guests and every plusixfive family member. Shocked and slightly (OK, very) sceptical that she had skills other than swiping leftovers, we decided to give her a chance.

And boy did she prove me wrong with these sardine puffs. Incredibly easy to make yet packed full of flavour, for me every bite brings back memories: it's swelteringly hot in the Catholic High School canteen, recess bells are chiming, I am the geeky, awkward kid wearing too-short shorts, and musky, sweaty schoolboys are eagerly queuing up for fried chicken wings and sardine puffs, spewing flakes of puff pastry everywhere.

PHOEBE: A hotel valuer by day, I travel to some of the world's fanciest hotels and resorts to determine how much they are worth (yes, it is a real job). On the weekends I run a little vintage cake and furniture store called Carpenter and Cook with some friends, and my main role is to stock the store with interesting vintage furniture and homewares, i.e. I shop for the shop!

Sometime in the autumn of 2011, a bunch of my friends and I organised a getaway in a small forest cottage near the border of Wales and Gloucestershire. Goz, a one-man cooking machine, tagged along for this holiday and one day for dinner, in the span of a few hours, produced the best lor arkh (Teochew braised duck) I've had in a very long time. I was hooked! I plotted and schemed thereafter to get onto the roster as a plusixfive crew member, as I was too cheap to pay for a legitimate seat at the much-coveted supper club.

The only way was to work for my food. However, there was one obstacle. Word on the street was, only young and nubile females need apply and Goz would handpick the most beautiful to be part of his elite group of fronts of house. How I finally made it through the door to Goz's Studio 54 remains a mystery. Was it the promise of my sardine puff recipe or the excuse that I needed to gain waitressing experience for my store that appealed to his charitable nature? Who knows! The most important thing is that I got free access to this famous supper club in the middle of central London a million miles away from home. I left the little flat on that warm Sunday night with all the takeaway boxes I could carry, stuffed full of chap chye, rice wine chicken, chwee kueh and rendang—and a head full of new schemes to stay on that roster for as long as such delicious food was being served out of that teeny tiny kitchen.

PHOEBE: This is a super scrumptious afternoon snack I used to eat growing up. One day in London I suddenly developed a real craving for these and learned how to make them by trial and error. I'd never realised how simple they were to make until then. The trick is to make sure that, when scooping the sardine mixture onto the pastry, it is not too wet and sloppy as the pastry has to be as dry as possible. And also, don't be too greedy and overstuff it because the filling may leak or 'explode' when baked!

SARDINE PUFFS

Mashed Sardines with a Hint of Chilli Baked in Puff Pastry

MAKES ABOUT 18

FILLING

1 (300-g) can sardines in tomato sauce

3 shallots, finely chopped

3 fresh red chillies, finely chopped

2 cloves garlic, finely chopped

Zest and juice from 4 limes

2 tsp Tabasco sauce

2 tbsp ketchup

3 tbsp sweet chilli sauce
  (I use Linghams brand)

1 tsp ground white pepper

500 g puff pastry

1 egg yolk

Roughly mash all the ingredients for the filling in a large bowl with the back of a fork until well-combined. Let sit in the fridge, covered, to marinate for at least 3 hours.

Roll out the puff pastry to about 2 mm thick and cut into 10-cm squares. You can make them bigger if you want. Working quickly, place a teaspoon of sardine filling in the middle of each pastry square. Dab a bit of water along the edges before folding into a triangle. Press down on the edges with a fork to seal, creating a simple pattern. Place the sardine puffs in the fridge for about 30 minutes to firm up.

Preheat the oven to 220°C. Beat the egg yolk. Using a pastry brush, lightly brush the egg yolk over the sardine puffs. Bake in the top rack of the oven for about 7 minutes, or until the pastry puffs up and becomes golden brown. Then flip the sardine puffs over, lightly brushing with the egg yolk and baking for an additional 7 minutes, or until the pastry puffs up and becomes golden brown. Serve and consume immediately.

SHU HAN: *Otak* literally means 'brains' in Indonesian and Malay. Thankfully though, this probably just describes the soft, mousse-like texture of this spicy fish paste, and has nothing to do with the grey matter of fish. Otak otak takes quite a bit of effort but I can't imagine a weekend barbecue or a plate of nasi lemak without it, and the fragrant, charred results are often delicious enough to bribe your friends into helping you anyway.

OTAK OTAK

Grilled Spicy Fish Paste Wrapped in Banana Leaf

MAKES 30–40

REMPAH (SPICE PASTE)

1 kg shallots

15 dried red chillies, soaked in lukewarm water for 1 hour

8 candlenuts or macadamia nuts

1 (3-cm) piece galangal

2 tbsp belacan (dried shrimp paste), toasted (see page 43)

3 tbsp ground coriander

1½ tbsp ground turmeric

4 tbsp groundnut or coconut oil

3 tbsp sugar

1 tsp sea salt

FILLING

1.5 kg mackerel fillets

8 eggs

400 ml coconut milk

8 kaffir lime leaves

2 tbsp cornstarch

40 (20 by 12-cm) banana leaves

To make the rempah, blend the shallots, chillies, candlenuts, galangal, belacan, coriander and turmeric in a food processor or pound with a mortar and pestle until a smooth paste is formed. Heat the oil in a wok and fry the rempah over medium heat. The rempah will start off watery, but be patient and slowly fry it as you want the paste to be dry and the flavours to intensify. Add the sugar and salt. Remove the wok from the heat when the oil separates and the rempah becomes intensely fragrant, about 30 minutes. Set aside to cool.

Scrape the meat off the mackerel fillets, being extra careful to leave behind the bones and skin. Blend the meat in a food processor or chop it finely until a smooth paste is formed. Beat the eggs and coconut milk in a bowl until well-combined. Add the fish paste, kaffir lime leaves, tapioca flour and rempah and mix well. The consistency of the mixture should resemble that of pancake batter.

Soak the banana leaves in hot water for 5 minutes until soft. Drain and wipe dry. Place each leaf on a clean work surface, with its veins running vertically, making it easier to fold. Scoop 2–3 tablespoons of the filling onto the middle of each leaf, and spread it evenly so that it forms a rectangular strip about 5 mm thick. Fold one side of the leaf over the filling, covering it fully, followed by the other side, creating a long, slender parcel. Create a fold about 1 cm from the ends to keep the paste from spilling out. Secure with toothpicks.

Grill the parcels in an oven preheated to 250°C with the folds facing up (as the filling may expand and burst open) or on your oven's grill setting, or—the best way to do it—over a hot barbecue, flipping once, for about 10–15 minutes, or until the banana leaves are wonderfully burnt. Serve as a side with nasi lemak or laksa, or just dig in as is.

BRAINS

SHUWEN

Two Hungry Girls is a pair of friends who draw inspiration from their heritage and travels to bring creative Chinese cuisine to hungry Londoners through pop-up events, supper clubs and classes. Shuwen Tan, an effervescent, melodramatic and wildly animated little firecracker (aka a regular Peranakan lady), is one half of this duo. She is Chinese, was born in Malaysia, and is out to show that Chinese food is so much more than just takeaway that comes in a box after a big night out. I got to know Shuwen through Leigh, the other half of Two Hungry Girls, who dropped by as a guest at one of my suppers before they started their droolsome twosome.

SHUWEN: I got to know Goz through the supper club scene in London, and have had the pleasure of collaborating with him and plusixfive on many a food event. His fun-loving attitude and true enjoyment of food and meeting people is infectious.

I'm a self-taught cook whose favourite food comes from my own heritage: Chinese and Southeast Asian cuisine. Currently working in food event design, I also get my hands dirty testing food products, as well as doing recipe development and food styling.

More often than not, people in the UK don't have the best perception of Chinese food. It's seen as greasy takeout after a big night out or a down and dirty meal served by rude wait staff. My mission is to change this view and show how exciting, varied and culturally rich Chinese cuisine can be. To that end, I co-founded the Two Hungry Girls supper club, which specialises in traditional and contemporary dishes.

SHUWEN: During some very memorable travels to Laos, I came across these lemongrass skewers stuffed with minced pork. They looked so attractive, I didn't need to taste them to decide I wanted to recreate them at home. They are best cooked under the grill or over the barbecue, their fragrant, zesty aroma always filling the room and making me smile. A great ice-breaker at a supper club or dinner party (as everyone always tries to figure out how best to break into them), these skewers work well as appetisers.

LEMONGRASS PORK SKEWERS

MAKES 8

250 g minced pork

4 cloves garlic, finely chopped

1 (5-cm) piece fresh ginger, grated

3 water chestnuts, finely chopped

2 stalks lemongrass, hard outer parts removed and very finely chopped, plus 8 additional for skewers

Handful of Thai basil leaves, finely chopped

2 tbsp fish sauce, or to taste

1 tbsp Shaoxing rice wine

1 tbsp brown sugar

Vegetable oil, for grilling

Lime wedges, to serve

Mix the minced pork, garlic, ginger, water chestnuts, 2 stalks of lemongrass, basil, fish sauce, rice wine and sugar in a large bowl, stirring until well-combined. Let sit in the fridge, covered, for at least 30 minutes or overnight.

To assemble, bash the thickest part of the lemongrass stalk, about 1–2 cm from the end, with a rolling pin. Pull apart the fibres of each lemongrass stalk to create a 'cage', and stuff with a ball of meat the size of a ping-pong ball. Ensure that the meat is encased in the stalk.

Preheat the grill to 200°C. Brush the skewers with vegetable oil and grill, turning at least once, for 20 minutes or until golden, nicely charred and cooked through. Season once more if required. Serve with wedges of fresh lime.

How To Stuff a Lemongrass Skewer

1. Pick lovely lemongrass sticks

2. Finely chop ingredients, mix into mince pork

3. Bash lemongrass bulb, to loosen fibres

4. Encase mince within open fibres

FEASTING
FOR THE
NATION

At the risk of getting (kueh)pie(tee) in my face, I will say this: Singaporeans are a quirky breed, especially the ones overseas.

Singaporeans spend an awful lot of time griping and ranting about Singapore: the heat, the rigid bureaucracy, the lack of freedom, arts, music and culture, and generally all things government related. So you would think that on the one day institutionalised by the government to celebrate and promote all things Singaporean, overseas Singaporeans would shun it like a plate of tasteless food-court chicken rice. But for some reason, whenever plusixfive advertises a National Day event, it goes viral and everyone gets all giggly and excited over it like a new-found food fad in Singapore.

In the summer of 2012, plusixfive was invited to host a dinner at the Supper Club Summit held at the Goethe Institute in London—an impressive and ambitious event that billed itself as the largest supper club event in the world, with over 20 supper clubs taking part. By happy coincidence, we were also allocated 8 August, the day before Singapore's National Day, to host our dinner. But since Singapore is seven hours ahead of London, it would technically be National Day in Singapore when we started our dinner.

Despite being the last supper club to sign up for the event, we were the first to sell out all 50 seats in less than four days with an extensive waitlist to boot, which even included officials from a Singaporean quasi-governmental body.

What's more, we told our guests that it was "red or dead", imploring everyone to wear red, one of the colours of the national flag, and boy did everyone make an effort! We had red-white dress combos, red ties, even someone claiming to be wearing red undies (we chose not to verify this)!

It might be uncool for Singaporeans to openly declare it, but they really do seem to love their country like a guilty secret (akin to harbouring a love for cheesy '80s pop tunes, or McDonald's Double Sausage & Egg McMuffin). Whatever it is, the number of Singaporeans who signed up eagerly for the event and who were on the waiting list will always warm the patriotic *hum* (cockles) of my heart.

We didn't just have random, homesick closet patriots in the house. We had old friends, colleagues, regulars and a few new faces of all nationalities, from Chinese to Italians. It was one noisy, wild, riotous mix. The best kind of mix.

I set the tone of the night by prefacing the meal with musings and nostalgic ramblings about home and family feasts (a large part of my growing-up years) and a little story about how the sound of a ringing bicycle bell always reminded me of bygone days, when the satay man would cycle around the neighbourhood, selling snacks and satay from a rickety, makeshift metal trough perched precariously on the back of his bicycle. Then I rang a little bicycle bell and right on cue, my friends hurried out from the kitchen, shouting "SATAY! SATAY! CURRY PUFF! CURRY PUFF!", cradling small wooden crates of banana leaf parcels containing fragrant pork belly satay, little bags of piping hot curry puffs (just like how I had them at school), and oil-stained packets of pillowy soft chwee kueh (reminiscent of the ones Mum brought home from Ghim Moh market on the weekends). Every dish served had a story linked to my childhood or that of the other volunteers.

8 August also conveniently fell on a Wednesday and, in keeping with the theme of nostalgia, we decided on a playlist of good ol' 1980s cheese pop tunes carefully curated by Lesley, our in-house, self-confessed "Queen of Mambo". Any Singaporean worth their salt in all things hip and cool would have grown up spending many a blurry Thursday morning nursing a hangover after partying at Mambo Night at Singapore's leading discotheque Zouk. Mambo Nights feature a catalogue of the best (and worst) tunes from the '80s and '90s, spun to rows and rows of pimply teenagers performing synchronised dances, gesturing every word of every song with their hands and arms as if they had all practised together the night before in their bedrooms (they probably had).

The supper club summit dinner was like a supper club mixtape of the greatest hits of plusixfive. For me, that one night was possibly, no, what am I saying, it WAS the best plusixfive dinner ever—gastronomically, musically and emotionally. It was everything I never dreamed plusixfive would become.

The supper club summit dinner was like a supper club mixtape of the greatest hits of plusixfive.

In Singapore, some ethnic groups share dishes as one culture invariably influences another in this melting pot of a city. Satay is a pretty good example. The spice mix very likely originated in Indonesia or Malaysia, as did the word 'satay'. However, as our neighbouring countries have a Muslim majority, they do not eat pork and their version of satay is commonly made with beef, chicken or mutton. On the other hand, it's almost sacrilegious to be a non-pork-lurvin' Chinese. Some Chinese dude somewhere probably scratched his chin and thought, "Hmm...there's chicken satay, lamb satay...but why no pork ah?" And thus the Chinese version of satay, made with pork, was born.

This recipe was featured in Ireland's *The Cork News* by the impossibly cute Irish television star Donal Skehan, who came by the supper club for our National Day extravaganza in August 2011. Friend and supper club regular Andrew Humphrey also used this recipe for his foodcart at the Redcar Rocks Music and Comedy Festival.

Ideally, you should prepare everything the day before you want to serve this dish. Also, thanks to the turmeric, your hands will be stained a gloriously bright Simpson yellow, so I would not make this the afternoon before a hot date.

CHINESE PORK BELLY SATAY

Smoky Fragrant Pork Skewers

MAKES ABOUT 30 (10-CM) SKEWERS

MARINADE

5 tbsp brown sugar

4 large white onions

1½ heads garlic

1 (7.5-cm) piece galangal

3 tsp ground white pepper

4 tsp ground coriander

4 tsp garam masala or any decent
   fiery and fragrant curry powder

4 tsp ground cumin

1 tbsp belacan (dried shrimp paste),
   toasted (see page 43)

1 tbsp sambal tumis belacan (page 118)

2 tbsp light soya sauce

4 tsp ground turmeric

6 stalks lemongrass

2 tbsp oyster sauce

2 tbsp vegetable oil

1 kg pork belly, skinless (get your
   butcher to remove the skin unless you
   have the knife skills of a ninja)

Blend all the ingredients for the marinade in a food processor until fine. Gradually add additional vegetable oil, one tablespoon at a time, and continue to blend until a nice, smooth paste is formed.

Slice the pork belly into 2.5-cm cubes. Submerge the pork in the marinade, getting your hands in there and mixing until every single cube of pork is covered in the wildly fragrant marinade.

Skewer the cubes of pork onto wooden skewers, leaving about half of each skewer pork-free for easy holding. Let sit in the fridge, covered, overnight to let the pork and marinade get intimate and kinky.

It's best to grill the skewers on a hot charcoal barbecue the next day. But if you live in the UK, and you don't fancy barbecuing in the rain, preheat the oven to 180°C and grill the skewers on each side for 10 minutes. Then give the skewers a good blast of heat at 200°C for a minute to get them nice and charred. Remove, serve and consume immediately. If your friends aren't impressed, change friends.

Jiu hu char literally means 'cuttlefish stir-fry', which is a bit of a misnomer as the predominant ingredient is grated turnip and carrot, and you can barely see the cuttlefish. This vegetable filling is perfect in a canapé starter. Packed full of umami from the dried mushrooms, shrimp, cuttlefish and charred pork belly, there are like a million ways to serve this. Well, okay, I lie. There are three ways that I know of—if you don't count eating it straight out of the wok as one.

JIU HU CHAR

Super Versatile Shredded Vegetable Filling

MAKES 1 SERVING

100 g dried shrimp (hae bee),
   soaked in lukewarm water for 4 hours

100 g dried cuttlefish

100 g dried shiitake mushrooms

Vegetable oil, for frying

250 g pork belly, thinly sliced

1 large white onion, finely chopped

1 head garlic, finely chopped

1 (2.5-cm) piece ginger, thinly sliced

500 g turnip or Japanese white radish
   (daikon), medium grated

200 g carrots, medium grated

2 tbsp Stock of Ages (page 46) or any
   pork stock

1 tbsp Shaoxing rice wine

2 tsp fish sauce

2 tsp light soya sauce

1 tsp dark soya sauce

1 tsp sesame oil

1 tbsp oyster sauce

2 tsp sugar

1 tsp ground white pepper

Soak the shrimp, cuttlefish and mushrooms in a small bowl of lukewarm water overnight, or for at least 4 hours. Strain, reserving the soaking liquid. Dry the shrimp, cuttlefish and mushrooms with a tea towel and slice the cuttlefish and mushrooms thinly. Set aside the mushrooms.

Heat some vegetable oil in a wok until very hot. Add the pork belly and fry over high heat for 5–10 minutes until the pieces start to brown and curl up slightly. Add the shrimp, cuttlefish, onion, garlic and ginger, and fry over high heat until mad fragrant.

Add the mushrooms, turnip and carrots. Turn up the heat and stir-fry for 10 minutes, stirring constantly. Resist the urge to add any water as there is already water in the vegetables. Frying will help to dry the vegetables out, intensifying the flavours and giving them a light, teasing lick of char.

Add the Stock of Ages, rice wine, fish sauce, light soya sauce, dark soya sauce, sesame oil, oyster sauce, sugar and white pepper. Add 2 tablespoons of the reserved soaking liquid. Continue frying for another 5–10 minutes, or until the vegetables are fully cooked. Make sure that the vegetables are not too wet and mushy, and do not overcook them as you want to retain some crunch and bite. Keep in mind that the latent heat from the wok will continue to cook the vegetables even after you turn off the heat. Season to taste.

TIP: You can easily make jiu hu char vegetarian or kosher by leaving out the pork belly, prawn and cuttlefish.

ON LETTUCE LEAVES

This is possibly the easiest and most fuss-free method. Place clean lettuce leaves (preferably round lettuce but iceberg lettuce is fine) on a platter. Heap some of the jiu hu char onto the leaf and top with a slab of pork belly. Garnish with a sprinkling of toasted white sesame seeds, coriander leaves and a squirt of Sriracha chilli sauce. Roll up your sleeves, roll up the lettuce leaf as you would a cigar and shove it into your mouth to consume. It will get messy.

HOW TO SERVE
JIU HU

POPIAH

You can also serve jiu hu char wrapped in a thin, egg-based, translucent pancake like a Vietnamese summer spring roll. We call the pancakes 'popiah skin' in Singapore but at the first supper club we served this, we made the mistake of asking the bewildered guests to "wrap the filling yourselves with your skin". Needless to say, it didn't really translate well. See page 92 for the recipe.

CHAR

KUEH PIE TEE

These make the perfect canapés as they are the perfect delivery vehicle for the flavour-packed jiu hu char filling, being small, bite-sized, feather-light and shatteringly crispy. See page 93 for the kueh pie tee cups recipe if you're one of the more extreme, obsessive-compulsive, adventurous people out there.

In Singapore, the popiah skin masters have a dense, sticky, elastic dough which is seemingly stuck to the palm of one hand. With a sharp, adept flick of the wrist, they slap the dough onto a smoking hot pan and as the dough snaps back up, it leaves a thin sliver of a crepe that cooks instantly on the pan, which the master then removes with the other free hand. All this happens in the blink of an eye. Tenacious Jason experimented tirelessly before coming up with the following perfect batter proportions and the perfect cooking technique for the amateur chef in a home kitchen. In Singapore, we often hold popiah parties where everyone assembles their own. Kinda like with Bloody Marys, everyone seems to think they can make a better one.

POPIAH

'Spring Rolls' Crammed with Jiu Hu Char

MAKES ABOUT 12

POPIAH SKINS

5 medium eggs

200 g all-purpose flour

Pinch of fine sea salt

350 ml water

2 tbsp vegetable oil

FILLING

Kecap manis (sweet soya sauce)

8 cloves garlic, crushed or pounded
into paste

200 g fresh red chillies, pounded
into paste (or use any good quality
store-bought chilli paste)

12 iceberg lettuce leaves,
washed and dried

1 small cucumber, peeled, deseeded
and julienned

1 large handful of bean sprouts,
tailed and lightly blanched

4 medium eggs, lightly beaten,
fried into an omelette and thinly sliced

Steamed Chinese lap cheong
(dried sausage), thinly sliced

1 serving jiu hu char (page 88)

Fried shallots (page 39), to garnish

Small handful of fresh coriander leaves
(cilantro), to garnish

To make the popiah skin batter, beat the eggs in a large bowl. Gradually sift in the flour and salt, and mix well. Add the water and oil, and stir to form a light batter—the batter should lightly coat the back of a spoon.

Lightly grease a large, non-stick pan with vegetable oil. Heat the pan over low heat. When hot, remove from the heat and pour a ladleful of batter onto the pan. Tilt the pan, spreading the batter evenly to form a layer thinner than a French crepe. Cook over low heat for 2–3 minutes, or until the popiah skin is cooked through and the edges begin to curl away from the side of the pan. Peel the skin off with your fingers, and transfer onto a plate. Separate each skin with a paper towel and cover the stack with a damp cloth to prevent them from drying out. Repeat with the rest of the batter, stirring each time before ladling, as the flour tends to sink to the bottom.

Plate all the ingredients for the filling separately so your guests can help themselves. Lay a sheet of popiah skin on a clean, dry plate. Spread about half a teaspoon of kecap manis, along with a little bit of crushed garlic and chilli paste in the centre of the popiah skin.

Add a leaf of lettuce, then pile the cucumber, bean sprouts, egg, lap cheong, and a heaped spoonful of jiu hu char onto the lettuce leaf. Garnish with a sprinkling of fried shallots and a few coriander leaves. The trick is to not be too greedy and stuff the popiah with too much filling. The skin is terribly thin and soft, so it tears easily.

Recall those hazy days spent in Amsterdam and roll that shiz up to form a fat cigar with the seam underneath. Trim off any excess popiah skin for neater presentation.

TIP: Cooked crab meat and prawns can also be used as toppings.

Kueh pie tee make really good canapés as the shells are a perfect delivery vehicle for the flavour-packed jiu hu char. They are bite-sized, feather-light and shatteringly crispy. Though Singaporeans often buy ready-made kueh pie tee cups, for the more obsessive-compulsive and adventurous out there, you can try making the cups yourself. This requires a special implement: the kueh pie tee cup mould. After brainstorming for days, we still cannot think of a worthy substitute in Western kitchen appliances. And yes, it looks like a medieval torture device. Though after half a day in front of spluttering hot oil making these bad boys (half of which will fail miserably), you will probably feel that they are actually a very modern torture device. Alternatively, you could substitute canapé cups, home-made or store-bought, though it definitely won't give you the same omfgwow factor.

KUEH PIE TEE

Crispy Canapé Cups Brimming with Jiu Hu Char

MAKES 40–50

60 g all-purpose flour

75 g rice flour

1 large egg

220 ml water

1 tsp vegetable oil, plus additional for frying

1 tsp fine sea salt

1 serving jiu hu char (page 88)

3 tbsp white sesame seeds, toasted (see page 43)

Handful of fresh coriander leaves (cilantro), to garnish

Sriracha chilli sauce, to garnish (optional)

To make the batter, mix the all-purpose flour, rice flour, egg, water, 1 teaspoon of oil and salt, until well-combined. Strain through a sieve to make sure there are no lumps. Let sit in the fridge for an hour to cool.

Fill a deep frying pan or wok with oil to a depth of 7.5 cm, or enough to submerge the moulds. Heat the oil until very hot. Test by dipping in a pair of chopsticks; when bubbles stream from the chopsticks, the oil is ready.

Dunk the mould into the hot oil for 2 minutes. Turn the heat down to medium. Remove the mould, dip it into the batter and lift immediately. The mould should be coated thinly with batter, which should sizzle slightly.

Dunk the mould back into the oil. The batter should puff up slightly. Give it about 40 seconds or so, before using the tip of a single chopstick to very gently and slowly nudge the cup from the mould. The cup should slide off, but as it is still soft, the mouth will close in on itself. A closed kueh pie tee cup is as useful as an inflatable dartboard. To prevent the mouth from closing, use the tip of the chopstick to prod the mouth, slowly spinning it to help it retain its circular shape.

Remove the cup from the oil when it is a nice shade of golden brown and let it rest on a paper towel to soak up the oil.

To serve, fill the cups with jiu hu char. Garnish with a sprinkling of sesame seeds, coriander leaves and a squirt of Sriracha chilli sauce. Consume immediately after plating as the cups will get soggy quickly.

Ngoh hiang was one of the dishes we served at our Singapore National Day event. I specially requested Jason make it because his version is kick-ass. Ngoh hiang literally means 'five fragrance', but I think it just sounds plain weird in English. You can find the same thing in Malaysia, where this tasty, moreish deep-fried pork roll is known as lor bak (which confusingly is also what Singaporeans call a dish of braised pork). It is called ngoh hiang due to the addition of five-spice seasoning (known as 'five fragrance powder' in Chinese) which goes into the marinade for the minced meat, giving ngoh hiang its signature aroma. To make matters even more mind-bendingly confusing, the term ngoh hiang is now used in Singapore to describe a whole smorgasbord of deep-fried foods, including fried prawn fritters, egg rolls, liver rolls etc., which are usually found in hawker centres served with a sweet, translucent, bright pink gloopy sauce which I've never quite understood. At plusixfive, we prefer it served with a drizzle of sweet black sauce.

Unlike the Teochew or Hokkien versions, the ngoh hiang featured here is the Peranakan version, which does not contain any yam or flour, so it is packed full of meaty protein and fewer carbs—great news if you are on the Atkins diet. Well, if you ignore the lard, that is. You could always wimp out and substitute lard with vegetable oil, which is healthier. Just don't let Jason's granny find out.

NGOH HIANG

Fried Pork and Prawn Rolls Wrapped with Bean Curd Skin

MAKES ABOUT 8

2 sheets fresh or dried bean curd skin (tau kee)

Vegetable oil, for deep-frying

1 tbsp cornflour, dissolved in 1 tbsp cold water

Kecap manis (sweet soya sauce), to serve

Sambal tumis belacan (page 118), to serve

FILLING

400 g pork belly, minced

150 g prawns, shelled, de-veined and coarsely chopped

100 g crab meat, cooked and shredded

100 g water chestnuts, finely chopped

2 spring onions, finely sliced

1 medium egg, lightly beaten

1 tbsp lard (page 44) or vegetable oil

2 tsp sesame oil

2 tsp light soya sauce

1 tsp dark soya sauce

2 tsp sugar

1 tsp sea salt

2 tsp five-spice powder

Freshly ground black pepper

Mix all the ingredients for the filling in a large bowl until well-combined. Let sit to marinate for at least 30 minutes.

If using dried bean curd skins, submerge them in a bowl of warm water for 30 seconds. Drain and gently wipe dry with a paper towel. Cut into 15 by 18-cm rectangles.

To assemble, lay the bean curd skins on a clean work surface. Place 3 tablespoons of meat filling along the long edge of each bean curd skin, leaving a small margin at each end. Roll over to enclose the filling, tucking in the ends as you go along to form a cigar shape. Smear some of the cornflour mixture along the seam and press to seal.

Lightly grease a steamer pot and plate with oil. Transfer the rolls to the steamer pot, placing them slightly apart. Steam for 10 minutes. Transfer the rolls to the greased plate and let sit to cool.

Pour enough oil into a deep frying pan or wok to submerge the rolls. Heat the oil until the temperature reaches about 190°C. Deep-fry the rolls in batches until they turn golden brown and crispy. Remove with a slotted spoon and let sit on a paper towel to soak up the oil. Cut into bite-sized pieces and serve with kecap manis and sambal tumis belacan.

JAMES

James Lowe is the hugely talented former head chef of the celebrated East London institution St. John Bread and Wine. He is also part of Young Turks, a chefs' collective which originally comprised Ben Greeno, Isaac McHale and James. Between them, they have worked at some of the best restaurants in the world. I confess, I am an unashamedly rabid fan boy of the Young Turks. Every pop-up food event that they have done has been nothing short of inspirational to me. Now they have all gone their separate ways: Ben is head chef of the much-lauded Momofuku Seiōbo in Sydney; Isaac is the executive chef of the consistently innovative and brilliant Upstairs at the Ten Bells and the newly opened The Clove Club, and James is doing pop-up events at various restaurants and pubs as he looks for a venue for his own gig. James had suggested contributing a simple char siew venison puff recipe, but I thought that was way too boring for a chef of James's talent, so I asked him for something more cheffy and crazy. He sure didn't disappoint.

JAMES: I got into cooking because I love being in restaurants. I decided I wanted to open my own and I thought that learning to cook would be the best way to achieve that. I put together a list of my favourite places and decided to work my way through them. After La Trompette and The Fat Duck, I spent four years as the head chef at St. John Bread and Wine, where I developed a strong food philosophy and love for British ingredients. It was there that I started to cement my ideas about the sort of food I wanted to cook for people—ultimately I decided that I wanted to cook the sort of food I enjoy eating. Most recently I have been cooking with Isaac Mchale as part of the Young Turks collective, which has enabled me to cook everywhere from East London to Taipei and Bogota.

I met Goz through his obsessive use of Twitter. It was hard to ignore him as he threw himself into it straightaway—a running theme,

it turns out! I went to one of the first plusixfive nights and was amazed, not just because the food was cooked in a domestic kitchen, but also because it was cooked by a guy who worked ridiculous hours every day of the week. I had a huge amount of respect for the fact that on his rare days off he'd decided to cook for 20-plus people in his home! I'd never had any of the dishes that I ate that night before, and on subsequent dinners the food always impressed me, either because it was new to me or because it was simply better than other versions I'd had. His incredible enthusiasm was admirable and infectious, as could be seen by the growing number of people he began to collaborate with.

It's great to have a friend whose food you enjoy eating and who you enjoy cooking for (when he gets his booking right) and it's a pleasure to be able to submit something for this particular work-a-holic's cookbook.

JAMES: Making your own blood cake is immensely satisfying. In fact, next to curing your own meats, it is the most satisfying thing I have ever made. You are totally transforming fairly rough-looking ingredients into something wonderful. This dish might also look quite odd at all stages of the process, yet what comes out the other end is fabulous.

SPICED BLOOD CAKE AND FERMENTED PEAR

Probably the Most Labour-intensive Dish in This Book. But Gawd Is It Delicious.

FEEDS 4–6

1 large leek, finely chopped

3 large carrots, finely chopped

4 brown onions, finely chopped

1 pig's head, de-boned

2 kg chicken stock (page 46)

800 g white onions

2 star anise

10 black peppercorns

8 whole cloves

1/4 stick cinnamon

1 nutmeg

20 Sichuan peppercorns

1 tsp fennel seeds

2 tbsp fresh thyme

1 tbsp fresh savory

3 bay leaves

Fine sea salt

800 g lardo

400 g preserved Chinese ham

2 kg pigs' blood

250 g semolina flour, finely ground

10 pears (Passe Crassane, Williams, Packham's Triumph or Beurre Hardy)

Watercress, to serve (optional)

Dandelion greens, to serve (optional)

Simple vinaigrette, to serve (optional)

TIP: You should buy and store the pears 2 weeks in advance, at room temperature. Don't allow them to get squashed or damaged.

Two days before serving, fill a large, heavy-bottomed pan with oil to a depth of 5 mm. Cook the leeks, carrots and brown onions slowly over very low heat, with the lid on, for an hour or until the vegetables have softened. Add the pig's head, cover with chicken stock and bring to a simmer. Preheat the oven to 100°C. Place the pot with the pig's head in the oven and braise for 5 hours, or until the meat gives and can be pulled apart. Remove from the oven and let sit to cool.

The day before serving, finely chop the white onions and cook slowly in a heavy-bottomed pan with the lid on. Grind the star anise, black peppercorns, cloves, cinnamon, nutmeg, Sichuan peppercorns, fennel seeds, thyme, savory and bay leaves in a spice grinder until fine. If the herbs and spices cause the mix to bind together, add some salt, which should help it to continue blending. Add the ground herbs and spices to the onions. Cook for an hour without covering.

Remove the pig's head from the stock and dice into 1-cm cubes. Dice the lardo and Chinese ham into 1-cm cubes. Combine the pig's blood, semolina and cooked onions in a large, heavy-bottomed pan and cook over low heat, stirring constantly (I can't stress this enough; it can catch very easily). Raise the temperature of the blood mix to 60°C. It should start to look slightly like porridge as it thickens. Once the blood mixture has reached 60°C, remove the pan from the heat and season to taste. You will need to add a fair amount of salt. As you add more salt, the flavour of the spices will really jump out at you, which is when you know it's been properly seasoned. Add the pig's head, ham and lardo, and stir to mix.

Preheat the oven to 100°C. Line some terrine moulds with a few layers of clingfilm, leaving PLENTY hanging over the sides. Ladle the blood mixture into the terrine moulds. **+**

+ Bring two sides of the clingfilm together, press and roll down, pushing out the air as you go. Fold the ends together and transfer the terrines to the oven. Bake for an hour. Remove, let cool and let sit in the fridge overnight.

Preheat the oven to 80°C. Place the ripe pears in the oven and bake until they reach 50°C at the core. The pears should retain the same shape, but their skins should brown and the insides should become a beautiful, slightly fizzy and ester-rich, juicy mess.

To serve, slice a piece of the blood cake and fry it in a non-stick pan on both sides, without any oil. It will burn easily. Don't make it too crispy and cook it just long enough for it to be hot. Slice a generous wedge of pear and serve it with the blood cake. Dress some watercress and dandelion with a simple vinaigrette to finish the plate.

MAINS

CRAZY LONG MENU

THAT TURNED A VEGETARIAN

As an impressionable kid, I used to see adverts on TV extolling the virtues of a fatless, saltless, sinless life. Compounded by the fact that I was a pimply youth who was ready to do just about anything to get into a girl's pants, I became a health-conscious nut (yes, believe it or not, this fine young man didn't always look like a tub o' lard), thinking that maybe if I had a six pack, women would fawn over me and feed me wine and grapes off their lithe bodies.

As part of the Adonification process, I used to scrape off all visible pieces of fat from any meat I was eating. One day, my mum cooked her signature pork belly with preserved vegetables. She saw my plate with its little mound of scraped-off blubber, and she looked at me as if she had caught me pants down monkey spanking. So I gingerly spooned pieces of quivering pork belly into my mouth and BAM. That was it.

Pork belly, braised overnight with preserved mustard greens and a small bunch of dried chilli for a little baby kick in the back of the throat. The fat and the meat had taken on all the flavours of the braising liquid and melted in my mouth. It was salty, sweet, garlicky, fatty and spicy all at once—hitting all the basic food yumminess receptors. This marked the beginning of the ruination of my Adonis-like figure. I sure as hell didn't get any love from the girls, but it was definitely the beginning of a long, lusty love affair with pork fat.

At one of our first plusixfive dinners, we served this signature dish of my mum's. We had cooked a special vegetarian meal for a lady who told us beforehand she was vegetarian. At the end of the night, she sheepishly confessed that she just couldn't resist picking at that pork belly. And this was after 20 years of vegetarianism! If that isn't a testimony to the awesomeness of fat, I don't know what is.

You should be able to find mui choy (preserved mustard greens) in your standard Chinatown supermarket. In Southeast Asia, most of the time it comes all semi-dried, wrinkly and speckled generously with salt or sugar, just laying there, uncovered. But in London, it comes vacuum-packed and sealed. If you're lucky, you'll find two versions, salty and sweet. I use the sweet version. If your local Asian supermarket doesn't have it, write to them and your local MP and boycott them with a vengeance. For the pork, go to your local butcher and get good free-range pork belly. That extra bit of cash you pay for happy pig meat is worth every penny. The intense marbling of fat doubles up as a courier of depth and flavour throughout the pork belly when it breaks down after the slow braising.

MUI CHOY KONG BAK

Braised Pork Belly and Preserved Mustard Greens

FEEDS 6–8

1.5 kg good-quality, free-range, marbled pork belly

3 tbsp five-spice powder

2 tbsp dark soya sauce, plus additional 2 tbsp

4 tbsp brown sugar

1 head garlic, finely chopped; plus additional 2 heads, crushed

1 tsp fish sauce

Vegetable oil, for deep frying

700 g mui choy (preserved mustard greens), preferably the sweet variety

4 tbsp Shaoxing rice wine

400 ml water

1 (2.5-cm) piece ginger

6 dried red chillies, soaked in lukewarm water for 1 hour

4 tbsp runny honey or maltose

1 stick cinnamon

2 tsp ground white pepper

Sea salt

Sugar

The night before serving, with any sharp implement, stab through the skin and the fat of the pork belly, but not the meat. Massage the pork belly all over with the five-spice powder, 2 tablespoons of dark soya sauce, sugar, garlic and fish sauce, really rubbing and getting it in there. Let sit, skin-side up and uncovered, in the fridge overnight for all those flavours to mingle and have a sexy time together.

The morning after, soak the mui choy in a bowl with sufficient water to cover. Let sit for 15 minutes. Replace the water, then let sit for another 15 minutes and repeat once more. Drain and rinse to wash away some of the salt—or else it will be way too salty. Chop into 2.5-cm chunks.

Add oil to a depth of 2.5 cm in a wok and heat. The oil is hot enough when you shove in a dry chopstick, and little air bubbles cling to and stream from it.

Drain the pork belly, reserving the marinating liquid. Be careful as you gently place the pork belly skin-side down in the hot oil —it will splatter and wheeze so use a splatter screen or wear suitable body protection. Deep-fry for about 10–15 minutes or until the skin starts to crackle and the fat starts to render, checking every couple of minutes. Flip the pork belly over so it's skin-side up. Add the reserved marinating liquid, mui choy, rice wine, water, 2 heads of garlic, ginger, chillies, 2 tablespoons dark soya sauce, honey, cinnamon and white pepper. Turn the heat to high and let it come to a boil. Once boiling, scrape off any bits stuck to the bottom of the wok, to ensure you don't lose any flavour. Turn the heat to low and simmer slowly for at least 6 hours, checking every other hour that there is sufficient water in the wok and that it's not burning. +

+ After at least 6 hours, season with salt and sugar to taste. I like this dish slightly sweet, but if you prefer it slightly salty, add more dark soya sauce. Then turn up the heat and boil it hard and fast for about 15 minutes, stirring continuously to ensure that it doesn't burn and that the sauce thickens slightly before lowering the heat to keep warm until ready to serve.

Remove the pork belly and slice. To serve mui choy kong bak the traditional way, ladle out a bed of mui choy and rest the pork belly on top. Then serve as a main with freshly steamed rice. To serve this as a starter, you can serve it between Christine's pillowy soft buns (page 110) with some crisp lettuce. I also occasionally like to serve mui choy kong bak as a starter on a bed of raw English lettuce cups, as the crisp freshness of the lettuce cuts through the richness of the dish.

Oooohyeahhhh.

CHRISTINE

Christine is a part-time actress, model, fashion journalist and full-time sweetheart all rolled up into one waif-like, indie-chic chick. We met through Twitter, when I was openly hunting for a front of house for my supper club after a friend pulled out last minute. I would like to think that she hopped on board thanks to my wit, charm and chiselled cheekbones, but I think it had more to do with the fact that I told her she could have full ownership over all leftovers from the supper club and a chance to meet tonnes of other crazed foodies.

One day, I decided to add kong bak pau to the menu: thick slices of mui choy kong bak sandwiched between soft, pillowy, clam-shaped buns. My mum used to make kong bak pau and we would get our buns frozen from Chinatown. When Christine found out I was about to use frozen buns, she reacted like I was going to commit heinous crimes on baby kittens. So since then, she has been the resident front of house and official bun-maker. The recipe that follows is Christine's grandma's recipe as remembered and adapted by Christine.

CHRISTINE: "The only Singapore supper club in London serving proper badass Singaporean food and dispelling the fiction that is Singapore fried noodles." This bio on Twitter is exactly what plusixfive is about and my first introduction to Goz and his supper club. Without any waitressing skills but a similar passion to show people what real Singaporean food is all about, I gladly helped out as the front of house on one occasion, which led to the next and the next until I soon became part of this big, happy, delicious plusixfamily. Plusixfive is more than just a supper club where we cook and guests eat their fill and leave. It is an experience, a gathering, a celebration of good times, literally.

Our guests have celebrated National Day with us decked in red, tossed yu sheng for the first time in their lives, revelled in Mid-autumn festival myths (as accurate as our memories serve us), and witnessed us dancing in the kitchen, aprons and all. We also had someone bring his friend over for a birthday meal once! Complete with birthday song with compliments from the team. As plusixfive's front of house, I can guarantee that no one leaves hungry or a stranger. And everyone also learns the truth: that Singapore noodles in all its garish, yellow curry-flavoured monstrosity is nothing but a big, fat lie.

CHRISTINE: My grandma's buns are soft, fluffy and moist. Exactly how I love them. I remember sitting on the floor, lined with newspaper, linen towels and plastic sheets, with her when I was a child. And on that very floor was where the magic began. Kueh, tarts, and of course, these buns. We made them together. Or rather, I tried to knead the dough with my little hands and she did everything else. To be honest, it took a while to remember the proportions she used, and I'm still not even entirely sure if I got them right. But every time I make these buns, I remember the times I had with my grandma, the way she used to laugh when I got flour in my hair. The way her gold tooth would sparkle in the sunlight with a chuckle. For me, these buns are what happiness tastes like.

MAN TOU

Steamed Buns for Mui Choy Kong Bak

MAKES ABOUT 20

STARTER DOUGH (MAKES 4 PORTIONS)

50 g all-purpose flour
150 g self-raising flour
½ tsp dry yeast
110 ml water

100 g all-purpose flour
200 g self-raising flour
30 g granulated sugar, or more if you like it sweeter
5 g dry yeast
160 ml whole milk
1 tbsp vegetable oil
1 portion of the starter dough (fully defrosted if stored in the freezer)

TIP: This recipe makes a fair number of man tou buns. But instead of reducing the recipe yield, for convenience the steamed man tou can be frozen and kept for about 3–6 months in the freezer. When you need them, just steam them up again!

To make the starter dough, mix the flours and yeast in a large mixing bowl. Make a well in the middle and slowly add the water in 2 equal batches, stirring after each addition.

Knead until a smooth ball of dough is formed. This batch of starter dough can be split into 4 portions and stored in the freezer until you are ready to make more man tou.

To make the man tou, mix the flours, sugar and yeast thoroughly in a large mixing bowl. Make a well in the middle, and place 1 portion of the starter dough in the well. Slowly add the milk and oil in 4 equal batches, mixing between each batch until a dough is formed.

Knead vigorously, dusting with flour as you go along, until the dough is smooth and does not stick to your hands. Cover with a damp tea towel and leave to proof for 45 minutes at room temperature. The dough should double in size.

On a clean work surface dusted with flour, divide the dough equally into 15–20 spheres roughly the size of a ping pong ball (or whatever size you prefer your man tou to be). Cover with a damp tea towel and leave to proof at room temperature for another 45 minutes.

To shape the man tou, dust your hands and rolling pin with flour. Press each ball with the palm of your hand until it's roughly the size of your palm. Dust flour on the surface and fold it in half so it forms a *D* shape. It should now resemble a flattened clam. After shaping all the pieces of dough, cover them with a damp tea towel and leave to proof for 1 hour. They should rise slightly. Steam each man tou in a bamboo steamer for about 10 minutes. They should all puff up beautifully and look fluffy and pillowy.

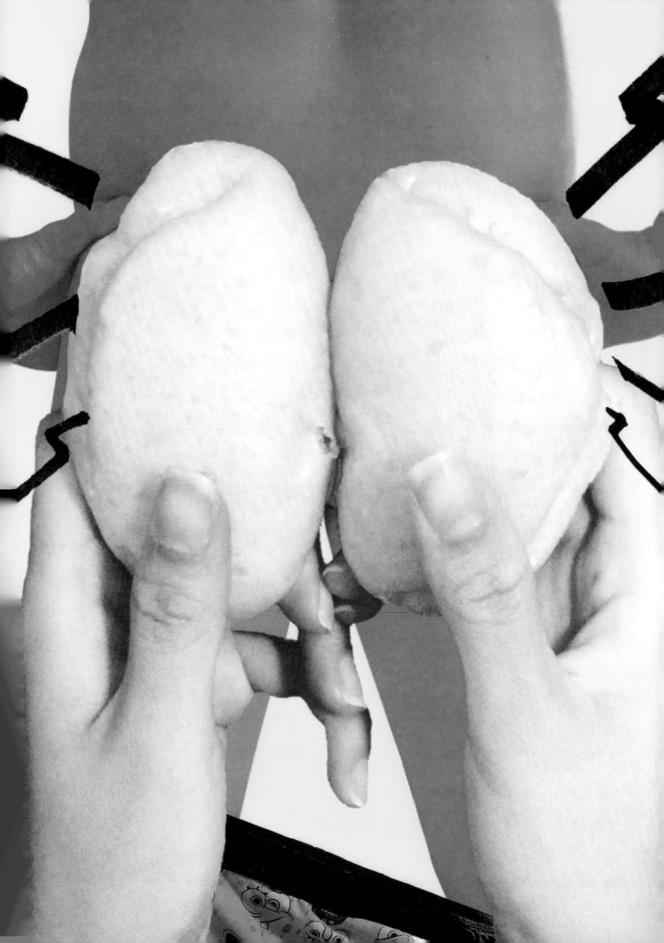

SHU HAN: Nasi lemak actually refers to coconut milk rice alone, but is often used to describe the rice served with all its side dishes as well. My friend swears it's not the same without otak otak or achar. All faff aside, I really only need the following for the most basic nasi lemak. It's a very simple but powerful combination of fluffy, fragrant rice with the nutty, salty aroma of toasted, crispy peanuts and ikan bilis (dried anchovies), and of course, that all-important sweet-spicy sambal tumis belacan. Add a couple of cucumber slices for a refreshing contrast to all that richness and spice, and an egg to round things off, and you've got my essential nasi lemak.

NASI LEMAK

Coconut Rice. The Perfect Sidekick to Any Curry or Saucey Dish.

FEEDS 4

2 cups long grain rice, such as basmati

2 cups water

1 cup coconut milk

6 pandan leaves, tied into a knot

1 tbsp sugar

2 tsp sea salt

1 cup ikan bilis (dried anchovies)

1 tbsp vegetable oil

1 cup raw peanuts, shelled with skins on, toasted (see page 43)

4 eggs

4 (A4-sized) banana leaves

Half a cucumber, sliced

Sambal tumis belacan (page 118), to serve

To prepare the rice, rinse the rice grains with water until the water runs almost clear. Cook the rice, 2 cups of water, coconut milk, pandan leaves, sugar and salt, in a rice cooker or in a saucepan on the stove according to the instructions on page 48.

Rinse the ikan bilis, drain well and dab dry with kitchen towels. Heat a wok over high heat and add 1 tablespoon of oil. Add the ikan bilis and fry until crisp and golden brown, about 8 minutes. Remove with a slotted spoon and drain on kitchen towels. Alternatively, spread the ikan bilis on a baking tray and toast in an oven preheated to 180°C for 25–30 minutes, or until dry, crisp and golden brown.

For the eggs, you have a choice of serving them hard-boiled and sliced in half, or go all out on the calorie front and serve them deep-fried in oil like my favourite nasi lemak hawker stall. Heat a pan over medium-high heat and add oil to a depth of 2.5 cm. When the oil is hot, crack in the eggs. Wait for them to set slightly before lightly ladling the hot oil over the tops repeatedly, letting them cook until golden and crispy on the edges.

To serve, scoop a portion of coconut rice onto each banana leaf and arrange the ikan bilis, peanuts, cucumbers and egg around the rice. Most importantly, finish off with a generous dollop of sambal tumis belacan.

TIP: Traditionally, broken local rice is used in nasi lemak. You can also achieve that dry, loose lightness with basmati rice. If using basmati rice, soak in water for 30 minutes beforehand for maximum fluffiness.

SIZZLING
SHIT-HOT

SHU HAN: When cooking, one often thinks of the delicious aromas, the brilliant colours of ingredients, and of course, the celebration of flavours on the tongue as one reaches in for one too many 'taste tests'. But I've always associated cooking with sounds. Every day as Mum got dinner ready, I would hear the noisy clatter of clogs against the kitchen tiles, the sizzling sputter of hot oil when vegetables were thrown into the wok, and the scary, loud clanging of the metal spatula hitting the sides of the wok. Food for me has always been an auditory, not just a tactile, experience.

I once made sambal at home and asked Mum for the blender. She passed me the mortar and pestle instead, and said it would be too much trouble to wash the blender. About 20 minutes into the pounding, the steady *thud thud thud* turned into a *thud groan sniffle thud*. My muscles were tired, and my face was streaming with sweat. I'm pretty sure I could have washed a lot of blenders in that time, and with less effort. That's my mum for you—coconut milk has to be freshly squeezed from hand-grated coconut, and rempah pounded by hand. I learnt a lot from that experience though. It made me realise how fully sensual cooking can be, how weirdly wonderful massaging marinade into chicken with your hands can feel, and how good washing rice feels when you use your fingers to swirl the grains around in the water.

I don't know if it's psychological then, but I find food that's *handmade*, always better. I guess the secret to my sambal lies somewhere in the couple of hours spent preparing the chilli paste and then patiently stirring it by the stove. I make extra each time I prepare this for a supper club, selling them at secret pop-up sambal sales in London. And on the jars, I write, 'Made with love, sweat and tears', because, I guess, that really is what goes into this sambal.

SAMBAL

SHU HAN: You will see this chilli used throughout the book. It's the secret ingredient that makes anything and everything taste good. Use sambal as the base for creating all sorts of Singaporean classic stir-fried noodles, barbeques, curries and sauces. That said, it's also an extraordinary side dip; nasi lemak is not nasi lemak and Hokkien prawn mee is not Hokkien prawn mee without a good dollop of this sambal chilli on the side. Due to popular demand (and a couple of death threats, poison darts, evil eyes and custard pies thrown our way from the sambal-hungry), Shu Han's Sizzling Shit-Hot Sambal was born. We decided to sell it online and did random, pop-up, covert sambal drops at various locations in London. Here's the recipe, sweat and tears not included.

SAMBAL TUMIS BELACAN

The Only Chilli Sauce You'll Ever Need

MAKES 2 CUPS

1 (2.5-cm) cube belacan (dried shrimp paste), toasted (see page 43)

400 g shallots

30 dried red chillies, soaked in lukewarm water for 1 hour

4–5 large fresh red chillies

5 cloves garlic

2 stalks lemongrass

8 candlenuts or macadamia nuts

½ cup groundnut or coconut oil

3 tbsp tamarind pulp, soaked in 3 tbsp warm water

4 tbsp gula melaka (palm sugar)

Blend the belacan, shallots, dried and fresh chillies, garlic, lemongrass and candlenuts in a food processor or pound with a mortar and pestle until a smooth paste is formed.

Heat the oil in a wok and fry the paste over medium-low heat for about 10 minutes, stirring constantly so it doesn't burn. Add the tamarind pulp. Continue to fry until you see the oil separating from the paste, at least 30 minutes. (Yes, at least. Treat it as risotto practice.)

Add the gula melaka right at the end, allowing it to melt in the hot sambal before stirring to combine.

Let cool before storing. Sambal will keep, refrigerated, for about 1 month; the layer of oil on top keeps it from spoiling. Alternatively, sambal can keep, frozen, for months.

TIP: You can adapt this recipe, making it sweeter by adding more gula melaka or shallots; spicier by adding more fresh chillies or even bird's eye chillies; and more pungent by adding more garlic.

IKAN BAKAR (GRILLED FISH)

You can use most sorts of fish that are on the bone; mackerel works especially well. Cut slits on either sides of the fish, and rub with sea salt. Rinse an A3-sized piece of banana leaf and pat dry. (You can use aluminium foil if desperate, but I will judge you.) Smear sambal tumis belacan on the banana leaf. Place the fish on top and smear more sambal on the fish. Wrap the banana leaf and seal with toothpicks. Cook over a hot barbeque or oven grill for about 15 minutes, depending on the size of the fish, flipping once after 7 minutes. It'll be ready when you can smell the seductive aroma of grilled fish and burnt banana leaves. Finish with a squeeze of lime.

STINGRAY

Rub generously with sea salt, then set aside. Rinse and pat dry. A ray wing is really thin, so only grill for about 7 minutes, flipping once after 3 minutes. Sambal stingray is typically served with a tangy dip made of chopped red bird's eye chillies, a couple of thinly sliced shallots, 2 tablespoons of calamansi lime juice, 1 teaspoon of sugar and 1 tablespoon of fish sauce or cincalok (fermented shrimp paste).

TERUNG (EGGPLANT)

Traditionally, eggplant is fried in a sinful amount of oil, but there's a simpler way to go about it without getting your face greasy. Grilled, the eggplant (aubergine) takes on a delicious smokiness and its skin a dark glossy sheen, while its insides turn into a creamy pulp, a happy sponge soaking in the spicy chilli. Slice a medium eggplant into rounds. Combine 2 tablespoons of oil with 2 teaspoons of fish sauce and a pinch of sugar, and brush this all over the eggplant slices. Preheat your grill or oven to 200°C. If using a grill, grill for 10–15 minutes until tender, flipping once. If using an oven, bake for 20 minutes, flipping once. Smother with sambal tumis belacan to finish.

UDANG (PRAWN)

This recipe is simple, but the sauce is almost addictive. Fry 4 tablespoons of sambal tumis belacan in some oil until fragrant. Add 600 g of peeled prawns and fry for a couple of minutes until just pink. Add 4 tablespoons of tamarind juice, 1 tablespoon of soya sauce and 2 teaspoons of sugar. Simmer until the prawns are fully cooked. To serve, garnish with thinly sliced kaffir lime leaves and chopped fresh coriander leaves (cilantro).

BAL

KANGKONG

I usually add a couple of chopped red bird's eye chillies to this dish, but if you're already sobbing at the spiciness of my sambal tumis belacan, skip this step. Trim the tough stems off 300 g of kangkong (morning glory). In a screaming hot wok, add 2–3 tablespoons of oil. Fry a handful of soaked dried shrimp (hae bee) with 1 tablespoon of minced garlic and 1 tablespoon of shallots, along with 2 tablespoons of sambal tumis belacan and the extra red bird's eye chillies. When fragrant, add the kangkong with a large pinch of sugar and salt to taste. It's ready when the leaves are wilted and the stems are tender but still crunchy.

NOTES: We also did this with other British leafy vegetables that are in season: beet leaves in summer, and Swiss chard in fall.

SHU HAN: This is one of my signature sambal dishes. There's nothing better than cutting into a hard-boiled egg from a happy hen to reveal creamy orange yolks. Well, nothing better except that same egg, deep-fried to create a crisp golden surface, then smothered with sambal.

SAMBAL TELUR

Deep-fried Eggs Coated with Sambal

FEEDS 12

12 large free-range eggs

Vegetable oil, for frying

1 cup sambal tumis belacan (page 118)

Fresh coriander leaves (cilantro),
  to garnish

For perfectly cooked eggs, place room-temperature eggs in a single layer in a saucepan with enough cold water to cover. Bring to a boil over high heat. Once boiling, remove the pan from the heat and let the eggs sit in the hot water for 6 minutes. Immediately transfer the eggs to a bowl of ice-cold water. This ensures you don't get those horrible grey sulphurous rings around the yolks; the whites will be firm but the yolks will not be fully cooked yet. Peel when cool enough to handle, then pat dry.

Heat the oil in a wok and deep-fry the eggs until golden on the outside. Drain and set aside. That golden jacket around the egg isn't just for show; besides adding a crispy fragrance, it ensures that the yummy sambal sauce clings to the egg.

Heat the sambal tumis belacan in a small pan over medium heat until hot. Gently toss the eggs in the sambal to coat. To serve, sprinkle chopped coriander leaves for a bit of greenery if you like.

SHU HAN: I hate to call sayur lodeh a mixed vegetable curry, because it is so much more than that. For one, this is not a random combination of the sorry bits of vegetables sitting in your fridge. The vegetables are all there for a reason, whether to sweeten the broth, give bite and texture, or act as a sponge for soaking up all the lovely juices that are squirted all over the insides of your mouth when you bite into them. In fact, for those used to the fiery, pungent spices of your neighbourhood Indian restaurant, the gentle, mild flavours of this Indonesian dish might seem kind of wimpish for a curry. I like to think of it instead as a light yet rich vegetable stew, simmered with fragrant herbs and spices and laced with sweet, creamy coconut milk.

SAYUR LODEH

Light Vegetable Curry Stew

FEEDS 6–8

250 g long beans or green beans

1 large carrot

Half a white cabbage

1 medium eggplant (aubergine)

Tau pok (fried bean curd) (optional)

2 tbsp vegetable oil

400 ml coconut milk

3 kaffir lime leaves

Sea salt

Sugar

Lontong (pressed rice cakes) (optional)

Sambal tumis belacan (page 118) (optional)

REMPAH (SPICE PASTE)

15 dried red chillies, soaked in lukewarm water for 1 hour

150 g shallots

5 candlenuts or macadamia nuts

5 cloves garlic

1 (5-cm) piece ginger

1 (5-cm) piece galangal

1 (1-cm) cube belacan (dried shrimp paste), toasted (see page 43)

1½ tbsp dried shrimp (hae bee), soaked in lukewarm water for 4 hours, reserving the soaking liquid

1½ tbsp ground turmeric

3 stalks lemongrass

Rinse and chop the vegetables and tau pok. There is no need for geometric accuracy, but the beans should be about finger-length, and the rest cut into similar-sized chunks, so that they cook in roughly the same amount of time.

Blend all the ingredients for the rempah in a food processor or pound with a mortar and pestle until a smooth paste is formed. Heat the oil in a wok and fry the rempah over medium heat until the oil separates and the rempah becomes intensely fragrant, about 30 minutes.

Add the coconut milk, kaffir lime leaves, reserved shrimp-soaking liquid and enough water to cover. Bring to a boil. Add the vegetables and simmer until very tender but not mushy.
Add more water if necessary to achieve your desired consistency; I like mine slightly thicker. Season with salt and sugar to taste.

Add the tau pok and lontong, and the sambal if you're a spice fiend. The lontong will make this a more substantial one-pot meal, but don't worry if you can't get them; just serve over generous bowls of freshly steamed rice.

I like to serve dishes that challenge people's gastronomic preconceptions. Chap chye is a perfect example. It is essentially a stir-fry, which people think of as being very cheap, easy and simple to make—throw vegetables in a wok, flick it around on high heat, add soya sauce and oyster sauce and serve. But Peranakans are well-known for overcomplicating things, and in the process they've magnified the dish's awesomeness exponentially. Unlike a Chinatown stir-fry, this dish is meant to be almost soup-like. The vegetables should be swimming in gravy and this is because, if you've used a good, rich stock base, you will have your guests wanting to slurp up that gravy intravenously.

CHAP CHYE

The Vegetable Stir-fry to End All Stir-fries with Gravy as Addictive as Crack

FEEDS 6–8

1 tsp sesame oil

2 tsp vegetable oil

Half a head garlic, skinned and finely chopped

1 (1-cm) piece ginger, skinned and finely chopped

1 large onion, finely chopped

100 g dried shrimp (hae bee), soaked in lukewarm water for 4 hours

200 g pork belly or pork neck, thinly sliced

1 (20-cm) Japanese white radish (daikon), cut lengthwise into quarters and sliced 5 mm thick

1 cabbage, cut into 2.5-cm chunks

3 carrots, cut lengthwise into quarters and sliced 5 mm thick

30 g dried wood ear fungus, soaked in lukewarm water for 4 hours and thickly sliced

100 g dried shiitake mushrooms, soaked in lukewarm water for 4 hours and thickly sliced, reserving the soaking liquid

700 ml Stock of Ages (page 46)

Few tbsp Meat Shreds (page 46) (optional)

50 g glass rice noodles (tang hoon)

50 g dried bean curd skin (tau kee), broken into 7.5-cm pieces

2 tbsp tau cheo (fermented soya bean paste)

1 tsp light soya sauce

1 tbsp fish sauce

2 tbsp Shaoxing rice wine

1 tsp oyster sauce

1 tsp kecap manis (sweet soya sauce)

1 tsp sambal tumis belacan (page 118)

In a small bowl, add the tau cheo, light soya sauce, fish sauce, rice wine, oyster sauce, kecap manis and sambal tumis belacan. Mix well and set aside.

Heat a large wok over high heat until smoking hot. Add the vegetable oil and sesame oil. Fry the dried shrimp, garlic, ginger and onion until fragrant. Add the pork belly and fry briskly for 5 minutes.

Add the daikon and carrots. Stir-fry for 8–10 minutes, stirring constantly so the vegetables don't burn, until light brown in colour. Add the wood ear fungus, shiitake mushrooms and cabbage. Turn up the heat very high and continue to fry the vegetables for another 8–10 minutes. This is to ensure that all the vegetables get the proverbial 'wok hei'—the faintly smoky fragrance one gets from a combination of the slight charring and searing of food in the intense heat of a seasoned wok. Once the vegetables start to soften and colour, add the dried bean curd skin, Stock of Ages, Meat Shreds, sauce mixture and 50 ml of the reserved mushroom soaking liquid.

Reduce the heat to medium, cover and simmer for 15 minutes. Check periodically to ensure it isn't drying up and top up the stock if necessary; the vegetables should be swimming in stock. When cooked, the vegetables should be soft yet retain their bite. If the vegetables are too hard, simmer for another 5–10 minutes.

Add the glass rice noodles, ensuring they are submerged in the stock, and cook for 5 minutes. Turn off the heat and let sit for all the ingredients to absorb the rich, explosive tastiness of the stock.

Season the stock to taste. If you like it spicy, add in more sambal tumis belacan. If you prefer a bit of sweetness, add more kecap manis. For saltiness, you can add in more fish sauce or soya sauce. To serve, remember to ladle buckets of gravy over the vegetables and glass rice noodles. Don't be surprised if your guests start drinking that kickass gravy like a soup!

MARCUS

My love affair with Peranakan food became serious after I got to know Marcus. His mum, Aunty Su, runs Blue Ginger Restaurant, a culinary stalwart in Singapore's foodie scene. Prior to meeting him, I had never really eaten real, homemade Peranakan food. So when I first tasted his mum's ridiculously fabulous cooking, it was like losing my virginity all over again. My tastebuds were blown right open to a completely new landscape of flavours as I experienced all kinds of intense umami hits. I'd never have dreamt this was possible in seemingly simple dishes like chap chye or bakwan kepiting, which look like simple stir-fried vegetables and a clear, plain meatball soup respectively.

I got to know Marcus in my twenties, and our mutual respect for each other's obsession with wine, women, song and such fuelled our spiral into all manners of debauchery. Fast forward a couple of years and despite my retirement from all that when I moved to London, Marcus and I somehow remained firm friends, most likely through our love of good banter and great food. I don't know many people I can chat to about food nonstop for hours on end, brainstorming for ideas and concepts.

MARCUS: One of the greatest misconceptions about being Peranakan is that you're an exotic ethnic mix (like half Caucasian and half Asian). Therefore you're unlikely to attract the ladies the way George Clooney and Richard Gere do. But what the Peranakan male does possess is an uncanny palate and nose for good food. So you can probably guess that most of my childhood was spent watching chefs and cooks go about their business, be it at Newton Hawker Centre or at Pete's Place at the Hyatt Hotel, rather than learning how to romance the ladies.

Goz was an elusive man when we were both budding, wannabe lawyers at law school in Singapore—all I heard were whisperings of his existence. It was not until we were about a month into our course that I was introduced to the legend. When Goz moved to London, breaking many a lady's heart in the process but setting off a flurry of new ones across the pond, he developed a sudden urge to spend all his waking weekends researching and cooking the Singaporean food from his childhood. Thus plusixfive was given life, like some weird Singaporean restaurant love child. During one of my trips to London, Goz mooted the idea of doing a collaboration between his supper club and Blue Ginger Restaurant, which is my mother's pride and joy. Both plusixfive and Blue Ginger were born from a desire to share, through food, a unique Singaporean culture. Goz's idea sounded great to me, and so I brought over some necessary ingredients and did my faithful best to recreate, in Goz's Islington crib, some of the offerings that are available at Blue Ginger. And behold, my mum's famous ayam panggang was reborn!

MARCUS: I chose to contribute a recipe for ayam panggang because Goz and I had such fun cooking it, we felt it would be a worthy entry into the annals of culinary history. It's also one of my mother's favourite recipes from the Blue Ginger restaurant and I thought she would be super pleased to know that it has been immortalised in print. One tip I have is to buy the best chicken you can afford. This may sound cliché, but those organic chooks, which have been living a carefree life, grazing on worms and bits of plants whilst roaming free around the vast plains, really do taste better than their battery-reared brethren.

AYAM PANGGANG

Char-grilled Chicken Smothered with Coconut Marinade

FEEDS 6–8

REMPAH (SPICE PASTE)

3 fresh red chillies

150 g shallots or small onions

4 candlenuts or macadamia nuts

2 stalks lemongrass, fleshy parts only and top third of the stalks removed

10 g belacan (dried shrimp paste), toasted (see page 43)

1 tbsp ground coriander

1 tsp ground turmeric

3 tsp sea salt

3 tsp sugar

1 tsp ground white pepper

2 tbsp vegetable oil

500 ml coconut milk

1 whole chicken, skin on and chopped into 10–12 pieces, or 10 chicken thighs with the skin on

1 stalk lemongrass, for basting

Fresh coriander leaves (cilantro), to garnish

Fresh red chillies, thinly sliced, to garnish

The night before serving, blend the ingredients for the rempah in a food processor, or pound with a mortar and pestle. Add the ingredients one at a time in the order they are listed, blending or pounding between each one until a smooth paste is formed. Mix the rempah and coconut milk in a large bowl. Add the chicken and let sit in the fridge to marinate, covered, for at least 12 hours or overnight.

The next day, at least 1 hour before cooking, remove the chicken from the fridge and let it come to room temperature. Meanwhile, fire up a charcoal or apple wood-fired grill. Alternatively, preheat the oven to 190°C on the oven's 'grill' setting.

Grill the chicken over medium heat on the charcoal grill for 10–15 minutes or in the oven for 25–30 minutes; keeping in mind that the breast meat cooks quicker than the rest of the bird. Smash a stalk of lemongrass until the fleshy part resembles a brush, and use that to baste the chicken regularly with the marinade while it's grilling. Meanwhile, simmer the remaining marinade over low heat for about 20 minutes, or until it thickens to the consistency of your desire. Remember to keep an eye on it and stir occasionally to prevent it from burning at the bottom.

When the chicken is cooked, let it rest for 1–2 minutes before slicing. To serve, pour the remaining marinade over the chicken and garnish with coriander leaves and fresh red chillies.

TIP: Cooking over too high a flame will scorch the chicken, leaving you with carbon-flavoured skin on the outside and raw meat on the inside. Cooking times will vary slightly depending on how thick your chicken pieces are, whether you are using breast or thigh meat and how cold it was before it came into contact with the fire.

YEN LIN

Yen Lin is a corporate lawyer by day and occasionally moonlights as resident front of house at plusixfive. You know that term 'finger on the pulse'? Well, she IS the proverbial finger on the pulse of all things hip, cool, and quirky in London. And when she is not busy gallivanting the streets of East London, or dancing the night away in an electro-pop costume at a rooftop warehouse party, she's my go-to girl whenever I need a cocktail buddy, an emergency shoulder to cry on, or someone to share general chitter chatter on work, women and woes. I lost my supper club virginity with her when she dragged me to eat at a stranger's loft in East London in 2010. It was that supper club which really made me seriously think about starting plusixfive. So thank you, chica.

YEN LIN: When I dragged Goz, literally kicking and screaming, to Ben Greeno's Tudor Road supper club in ultra-hip Hackney (insert long rant here over being forced to make small talk with skinny jeans-clad hipsters in Wayfarers), I think two things happened simultaneously that night: Goz lost his supper club virginity, quite definitively, and in the throes of the bacchanalia that ensued, the seeds of plusixfive were sown. In the times I have helped out at plusixfive as front of house since that fateful day, I have always been amazed and enthused by Goz's tireless and infectious knack for promoting Singapore's kick-ass food culture far beyond our manicured shores.

For my recipe contribution, I chose ayam buah keluak (aka chicken buah keluak), which I love. It's part of Chinese New Year tradition in my family,

and would likely be my death-row dish, narrowly edging out laksa. That said, I'm often stumped as to how to describe the flavour of buah keluak, or 'black nut', to the uninitiated. The closest thing, perhaps, is the bitter earthiness of the dark chocolate in a spicy Mexican mole...but MUCH tastier and more complex. When done the traditional Peranakan way, buah keluak is notoriously painstaking to prepare: it requires days of soaking, then the use of a cleaver (really) to chisel little openings in each walnut-sized nut, before harvesting the ink-coloured pulp within— way more effort than your average cook would risk his limbs for! This after the buah keluak has already been detoxified in ash or a running stream for 40 days to get rid of the cyanide. I salute the person who figured out this extremely detailed preparation. Seriously.

YEN LIN: Luckily for the lazy gourmet, it is possible these days to buy 'processed' buah keluak pulp which has been detoxified and de-shelled, shaving off a significant amount of prep time. The pulp also freezes well for up to a year. Purists may buy pre-cut empty shells separately to re-stuff their buah keluak, but this recipe does not demand it (shhh...don't tell your Peranakan grandma). Personally, I find the recipe works quite well without this step, which I usually skip to save time. Some prefer pork ribs to chicken or both, but whatever you do, make sure you keep the skin on and bones in, because it just tastes so much better that way.

LAZY AYAM BUAH KELUAK

An Easy Recipe for Peranakan Chicken and 'Black Nut' Stew

FEEDS 4

REMPAH (SPICE PASTE)

15 dried red chillies, soaked in
  lukewarm water for 1 hour

8 small shallots

1 clove garlic

2 stalks lemongrass

1 (2-cm) piece galangal

1 (2-cm) piece fresh turmeric
  or 3 tsp ground turmeric

2 candlenuts or macadamia nuts

1 tsp belacan (dried shrimp paste)

20 buah keluak

2 heaped tbsp tamarind pulp

Vegetable oil, for frying

4 chicken thighs, cut into large pieces

Pinch of sugar

Pinch of sea salt

Blend all the ingredients for the rempah in a food processor, or pound with a mortar and pestle until a smooth paste is formed. Set aside. Blend the buah keluak into a smooth paste. If using frozen buah keluak, add just a splash of hot water to soften before blending.

Mix the tamarind pulp with two small rice bowls of hot water. Strain to remove any seeds. Heat a generous glug of oil in a wok. When hot, add the rempah and fry, stirring constantly to prevent it from burning. Fry until incredibly fragrant, about 10–15 minutes. The oil will splatter and your fire alarm may go off at this point, but this is normal.

Add the chicken and coat evenly in the rempah. Fry for 5 minutes, or until slightly brown. Transfer to a large pot. Add the buah keluak and enough tamarind liquid to cover the chicken and buah keluak. Reserve any extra tamarind liquid. Bring the chicken to a boil with the lid on. Simmer over low heat for about 30–40 minutes, or until the chicken is cooked. Check in midway and stir, adding more tamarind liquid if necessary. Don't worry if it all looks like a black mess, this is normal. Remove the pot from the heat and season with a generous pinch of sugar and salt. Let rest for a few minutes, then serve hot with mountains of steamed white rice. Leftovers usually taste even better the next day.

JASON: My nan's ever-so-delicious kari ayam, or chicken curry, is yet another classic Peranakan dish that I grew up with. A very simple and popular Peranakan dish in both Singapore and Malaysia, those who are only familiar with the Indian madras or vindaloo will be surprised to learn that there is life beyond these plain-Jane takeaway curries. As in most other Peranakan dishes, the rempah (spice paste) plays an integral role, giving the coconut broth its gutsy depth and richness. The shiny, dark green curry leaves exude a distinctive nutty and citrusy aroma when gently fried in hot oil. Along with the cinnamon, cardamom and cloves, it contributes immense flavours to the finished dish. Although not the easiest ingredient to get hold of overseas, it can usually be found in all good Chinese supermarkets or in any Indian supermarket.

KARI AYAM

Light and Fragrant Peranakan Chicken Curry

FEEDS 4–6

REMPAH (SPICE PASTE)

10 shallots or 1 large red onion

6 cloves garlic

1 (2.5-cm) piece fresh ginger

2 stalks lemongrass

4 dried red chillies, soaked in
  lukewarm water for 1 hour

2 tbsp ground coriander

1 tbsp ground cumin

1 tsp ground turmeric

5 tbsp vegetable oil

3-4 sprigs curry leaves, stemmed

3 green cardamom pods, gently crushed

10-12 chicken thighs and drumsticks

2 medium potatoes, peeled
  and quartered

4 whole cloves

1 star anise

1 stick cinnamon

550 ml coconut milk

1 tsp sugar

½ tsp sea salt

Blend all the ingredients for the rempah in a food processor or pound with a mortar and pestle until a smooth paste is formed. You can add a drizzle of vegetable oil to aid with the blending or pounding if necessary.

Heat the oil in a wok and fry the rempah over medium heat, stirring constantly to prevent it from burning, about 5–8 minutes or until intensely fragrant. Add the curry leaves and cardamom, stir-frying for another minute. Add the chicken and potatoes, tossing to ensure everything is coated in that sexy spice paste. Add the cloves, star anise and cinnamon. Add the coconut milk and bring it to the boil. Add the sugar and salt, adjusting according to taste. Simmer over low heat, uncovered, for 40–45 minutes or until the chicken is cooked through and the curry sauce has thickened.

JASON: As one of the most famous Peranakan dishes, babi pongteh's significance is apparent from its vital inclusion in a traditional tok panjang, a formal dining experience adopted by the Peranakans for grand celebratory occasions such as weddings or birthdays. The feast is laid out on an immaculately presented table, and friends and family are invited to sample the culinary skills of the host. It is also a way for the household to showcase their wealth and fortune, as well as upbringing.

Unlike many other Peranakan dishes, the rempah (spice paste), which is often tedious to make, is very much absent here. Instead, the pork is braised slowly for a long period of time in tau cheo (fermented soya bean paste) and dark soya sauce to produce a wonderfully rich and sweet, tender meat. Babi pongteh is traditionally made with pig's trotters. The long stewing time breaks down the fat, giving the dish a succulent, gelatinous and smooth texture. If you cannot find pig's trotters or want a healthier take on this dish, pork belly works just as well. It is best made the day before as that gives time for the flavours to get all sexy overnight.

BABI PONGTEH

Slow-braised Pork in Fermented Bean Sauce

FEEDS 4–6

3 tbsp lard (page 44) or vegetable oil

20 shallots, finely chopped

1 head garlic, finely chopped

1 tbsp tau cheo (fermented soya bean paste)

1.5 kg pig's trotters, chopped into chunks

1 tbsp dark soya sauce

2 tbsp gula melaka (palm sugar)

650 ml water

Sea salt

Heat the oil in a wok over high heat until it starts smoking. Lower the heat. Add the shallots and garlic and stir-fry for 3 minutes, or until fragrant. Add the tau cheo and stir-fry for 5 minutes. Add the pig's trotters and cook for another 5 minutes.

Add the dark soya sauce, gula melaka and water. Turn the heat to high and boil, uncovered, for 1 hour. Then cover and reduce the heat to low. Simmer for another 2–3 hours until the pork is tender and the sauce has reduced and deepened to a very rich dark brown colour. Season with salt to taste. Serve with warm steamed rice or bread to mop up all that delicious stewing sauce.

YOLANDA

I have always known Yolanda was destined for awesomeness. Before she started her supper club, Wild Serai, she was already whipping up a frenzy of a Malaysian meal. You could smell her food cooking from down the road and you would literally follow your nose to her place. It was better than any Malaysian food I had ever eaten, even in Malaysia. I knew she had an itch to start a café or diner, so I offered her the opportunity to debut and guest chef at plusixfive. One thing led to another and now she is running her very own and very successful Wild Serai supper club. You go, girl!

YOLANDA: Fresh, aromatic and exotic, *serai* (Malay for lemongrass) is an essential ingredient in Southeast Asian and Malaysian cooking. Growing up in Malaysia, I recall being sent by my *nenek*, or grandmother, to pluck this wonderful herb that grew in wild abundance on grassy banks along deep ditches that collected and disseminated monsoon rainwater. Mission accomplished, I would run back to my grandmother's kitchen, gleefully clutching fistfuls of *serai*, *daun limau purut* (kaffir lime leaves) and *cili padi* (bird's eye chillies). Handing my prized possessions over, I would then squat on the kitchen floor and spend the next few hours watching her busily pound away at her gigantic *batu tumbok* (pestle and mortar), grinding spices, toasting belacan (shrimp paste) and doing all manner of wonderful things to produce a feast for the taste buds and the senses.

Our most memorable times as a family were always spent enjoying a huge feast around our dining table. Years later, while living abroad, I would find myself searching London's Chinatown for *serai*, only to find what grew wild and free in Malaysia selling at a premium! My supper club Wild Serai is a nostalgic celebration of the very best of Malaysian cooking, with a strong Nyonya influence. I do the cooking whilst my boyfriend, Sharif, is the organisational brains and manpower. He also sources the very best belacan possible (all the way from his hometown of Bintulu, Sarawak)! We had our supper club debut guest-chefing at plusixfive in late 2011, where we served up Malaysian chilli crab and king prawn sambal petai to a fantastic crowd. Since then, we've had a wonderful year of supper club adventures.

YOLANDA: The Portuguese landed in the strategic port of Malacca in Malaya in the 1500s and intermarried with the local Malay women—their offspring came to be known as Eurasians. The Portuguese came in search of precious spices, needed to marinate and preserve meat, and Eurasian cooking was perhaps one of the world's first fusion cuisines. The name 'vindaloo' is apparently derived from the Portuguese dish, Carne de Vinha d' Alhos, a meat dish usually consisting of pork that was marinated overnight in garlic and spices. The dish was modified with the addition of fiery red chillies and the use of vinegar instead of red wine. Our family version marries pork belly with chillies, garlic, ginger, fragrant curry leaves, mustard seeds, apple cider and balsamic vinegar. A complex layering of flavours—spicy, sour and slightly sweet—just the way Grandma Lucille used to make it.

EURASIAN PORK VINDALOO

Fiery Vinegary Pork Stew

FEEDS 6–8

1 kg pork belly, skinless, or pork loin if you prefer a less fatty cut

Sea salt

2 tbsp vegetable oil

30 curry leaves, or about 3 sprigs

50 g black mustard seeds

100 ml apple cider vinegar

4 tbsp balsamic vinegar or balsamic glaze

200 ml water

3 tbsp brown sugar

REMPAH (SPICE PASTE)

20 cloves garlic

25 g ginger

6 fresh red chillies, with seeds

15 dried red chillies (more or less depending on how spicy you like your vindaloo) soaked in lukewarm water for 1 hour

Preheat the oven to 130°C. Cut the pork belly into 5-cm cubes. Wash and rub with salt.

To make the rempah, blend the garlic, ginger, and fresh and dried red chillies with a little bit of water in a food processor, or pound with a mortar and pestle until a smooth paste is formed.

Heat the oil in a large cast iron pot and fry the curry leaves and mustard seeds for 3–4 minutes, or until fragrant. Add the rempah and fry for 5–8 minutes. Add the pork and brown for 5 minutes to seal in the juices. Add the apple cider vinegar, balsamic vinegar and water, ensuring that the meat is covered. Cover the pot with a lid. Slow cook in the oven for 3 hours, stirring every hour. Add the brown sugar during the last 20 minutes of cooking. If the curry is too sour or spicy, add more sugar to taste.

Let cool and refrigerate overnight to allow the flavours to intensify and get really robust. If you want to be ever so slightly healthier, skim off the excess fat after refrigeration and before consuming. Serve piping hot with white rice.

SHU HAN: Pig's trotters may scare some people off, but try them slow-cooked in this addictive, rich, sweet broth until they're meltingly soft and gelatinous, and see if you don't lick your sticky lips with satisfaction after that. This stew is favoured by all Chinese mothers during the post-pregnancy confinement period because it's incredibly nourishing, but I love this so much I once famously declared I wouldn't mind being pregnant just so I could eat this every day.

VINEGAR PIG'S TROTTERS

Syrupy and Tart Gelatinous Piggy Goodness

FEEDS 6–8

2 pig's trotters

500 g old ginger

5 tbsp sesame oil

1 (550-ml) bottle Chinese black vinegar (yes, the entire bottle)

1 cup brown sugar

Several hard-boiled eggs (optional)

Get your butcher to chop the trotters into large chunks for you, unless you have a giant chopper at home and the knife skills to match. If your butcher is nice, he may also help you shave or tweeze the hairs off, but if not, do it yourself. Boil the trotters vigorously for 15 minutes. Drain and rinse.

Roughly smash the ginger with the back of your knife. Fry the ginger in sesame oil over medium heat until fragrant. Add the trotters and brown them.

Add the black vinegar, sugar, and enough water to cover the trotters. Bring to a boil, then simmer over low heat for 2–3 hours. Alternatively, transfer to a slow cooker and cook on low for 4 hours. Add the hard-boiled eggs to the stew after the trotters are done.

TIPS: If you are using already-sweetened Chinese black vinegar, remember to adjust the amount of sugar accordingly.

Like a pickle, the flavours of the stew develop and intensify with time, and it tastes much better the next day, and much better the day after. The ingredients act as natural preservatives, so if you wish, do it the way our great-grandmothers did in pre-refrigerator days: make a big pot to be eaten throughout the week, bringing it to a rolling boil each time.

SHU HAN: Coffee might not seem like the most obvious pairing with pork, but you'll be surprised. The highly creative tze char chefs of Singapore have discovered that the bitterness of coffee strikes a perfect, delicious contrast with the sweet and savoury oyster and soya sauce clinging to the ribs. Usually made with plain, deep-fried spare ribs which are then coated in the coffee gravy, I make a version that is rubbed in the same spices, then slowly grilled so it's flavourful and fall-off-the-bone tender.

COFFEE PORK RIBS

A Tasty Collision of All Our Fav Things: Summertime! Barbecues! Coffee! Pig!

FEEDS 6–8

1 rack pork spare ribs

RUB

4 tbsp pure coffee powder,
  preferably freshly ground

8 tbsp brown sugar

2 tsp ground cinnamon

2 tsp ground coriander

Generous dash of freshly ground
  black pepper

Generous pinch of sea salt

GLAZE

2 tbsp strong black coffee, preferably
  made from freshly ground coffee

2 tbsp good oyster sauce
  (naturally fermented, msg-free)

2 tbsp dark molasses

Let the ribs sit until they reach room temperature. Meanwhile, mix all the ingredients for the rub in a bowl until the mixture is uniform in colour. Using your fingers, peel off the tough membrane that covers the bony side of the ribs. This is easier if you pull the membrane off in the same direction as the ribs—it will help to prevent the membrane from ripping as you're pulling it off the meat. Using your fingers, rub the meat really vigorously all over with the rub, trying to achieve an even coating.

Transfer the ribs to a bowl and cover. Let sit to marinate in the fridge for at least 12 hours or overnight.

Preheat the oven to 150°C. Lay the ribs, meaty side down, on 3 layers of aluminium foil, shiny side up. Cover with an additional 3 layers of foil and crimp the edges to seal tightly like a parcel. Grill in the oven for 2½–3 hours, flipping once halfway through. Alternatively, grill over low heat on the barbecue at about 110°C for 3 hours, flipping once halfway through.

When ready, the ribs should be tender and cooked, and the inner layers of foil should be kind of burnt. (You'll be glad I made you use 3 layers of foil.) Mix all the ingredients for the glaze until well-combined. The coffee can be quite bitter and overpowering, so adjust depending on how coffee-loving your guests are. Brush the glaze onto the ribs.

Turn the oven to its grill setting at the highest gas mark. Transfer the ribs to the oven, grilling for 2 minutes on either side. If doing this on the barbecue, place over the grill for a few minutes until bubbly, then flip over onto the other side, repeating until sticky and charred.

Let the ribs rest off the grill for 10 minutes before carving and serving. Cooking causes the proteins in meat to constrict and drives the moisture to the centre of the meat. Resting allows these protein molecules to relax and redistribute all that juicy awesomeness. Eat with your hands, and lick your fingers after.

you're lucky enough to own a smoker, one of
ipe testers, Ed Hall—also a long-suffering
of Goz's—smoked the ribs in his for about
rs at 100 °C. He didn't wrap them in foil as he
I them to be proper smoky. As a good rule of
, Ed's tip is that if you want to know if ribs are
ou should pick them up with a pair of tongs
e them a bit of a bounce or wobble. If the skin
at begin to break away, then they're done.
stay intact, you need to cook them a bit longer.

YUE LIN

Born in Singapore and raised in London, my little sister Yue Lin has always been the begrudging participant in my food experiments. She has helped me to cook at various church and supper club events, developing her own keen interest in cooking along the way. Despite the fact that she's now an adult and a practising lawyer, to me, she will always be that three-year-old girl on the beach, squealing and giggling whenever the tide rushed in over her little toes.

YUE LIN: One of my first forays into cooking Singaporean food took place overseas, when I was reading law in London. In our first year at university, my friends and I chose to celebrate our first Christmas with a decidedly Asian menu. Plans were made and ideas excitedly exchanged in between classes and online, and late at night while powering through tutorials.

When it comes to food, I must confess that I have no food loyalties or intense, homesick food cravings. That is to say, I don't trawl London with a fine-tooth comb in a bid to hunt down a particular restaurant serving char kway teow or have sudden midnight cravings for Rochor Road bean curd. But I do have a particular fondness for Hainanese food, especially my mother's fantastic Hainanese pork chops. So I decided that there was nothing I would like better on Christmas Day than a crispy, golden plate of juicy pork chops served with a side of tangy tomato sauce. And with that, I took my first real step into the realm of Singaporean cooking.

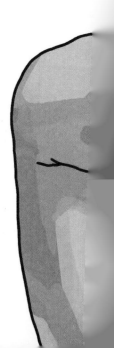

YUE LIN: This is my take on my mother's Hainanese pork chop recipe, which she, in turn, learned from her mother. It also includes a step for brining, which I picked up from various English recipes on how to flavour and tenderise pork chops. Using free-range, organic pork and really ripe tomatoes for this dish will yield the best results. The brining process takes between 12–24 hours so it is best if you plan a bit beforehand. The brining process moistens, seasons and tenderises the pork. You can skip that step if you are rushing for time but the pork will not have the same tenderness and flavour. I like to eat it with a steaming plate of white rice and with a serving of chap chye.

HAINANESE PORK CHOP

Deep-fried Pork Cutlet with a Rich Tomato Sauce

FEEDS 4–6

6 pork chops, about 5 mm thick

BRINE

18 g salt for every 300 ml water used

3 bay leaves

3 sprigs rosemary

2 tbsp freshly ground black pepper

SAUCE

20 tbsp tomato ketchup

3 tbsp oyster sauce

1 tbsp vegetable oil

2 large tomatoes, quartered

Half a large white onion, thinly sliced

2 tsp sugar

100 ml water

3 tsp cornflour, dissolved in 3 tbsp
cold water

Sea salt

Freshly ground black pepper

BATTER

20 Jacob's crackers, crushed very finely

Vegetable oil, for frying

2 eggs, beaten

Prepare the pork chops and brine 12–24 hours before cooking. To tenderise the pork chops, whack them with the flat of a heavy knife or a similarly heavy implement. To make the brine, measure the required amount of water by adding enough to completely submerge the pork chops in a deep bowl. Remove the pork chops and add the requisite amount of salt, about 18 g for every 300 ml of water. Stir until the salt dissolves. Add the bay leaves, rosemary and black pepper. If you have time, boil the brine for 30 minutes and let it cool completely to room temperature. This helps to squeeze out more flavour from the spices. Submerge the pork chops in the brine. Cover with clingfilm and let sit in the fridge overnight.

The next day, make the sauce by mixing the ketchup and oyster sauce in a small bowl, then set aside. Heat a small pot over low heat and add the oil. When the oil is hot, add the tomatoes and onions and fry until the onions are slightly transparent. Add the ketchup and oyster sauce mixture to the pot, stirring constantly. Add the sugar, stirring until the sugar has completely dissolved. Add the water and bring to the boil. Add the cornflour solution, then turn the heat down to very low and simmer for about 2 minutes until the sauce thickens. Season with salt and pepper to taste, then remove from the heat and set aside.

Drain and rinse the pork chops thoroughly. Dry with paper towels. Transfer the Jacob's cracker crumbs to a large, flat plate. Line another large plate with kitchen towels. Heat a pan over high heat, then add oil to a depth of 1 cm.

As the oil is heating up, dip the pork chops in the beaten egg, ensuring that every bit is covered. Roll in the plate of crumbs until completely covered. When the oil is hot, turn the heat down to medium and transfer the pork chops to the pan. Cook until golden brown on both sides. ✦

TIP: Be sure to periodically remove any charred crumbs from the pan. You might also want to change the oil if it turns a very dark brown as you fry your pork chops.

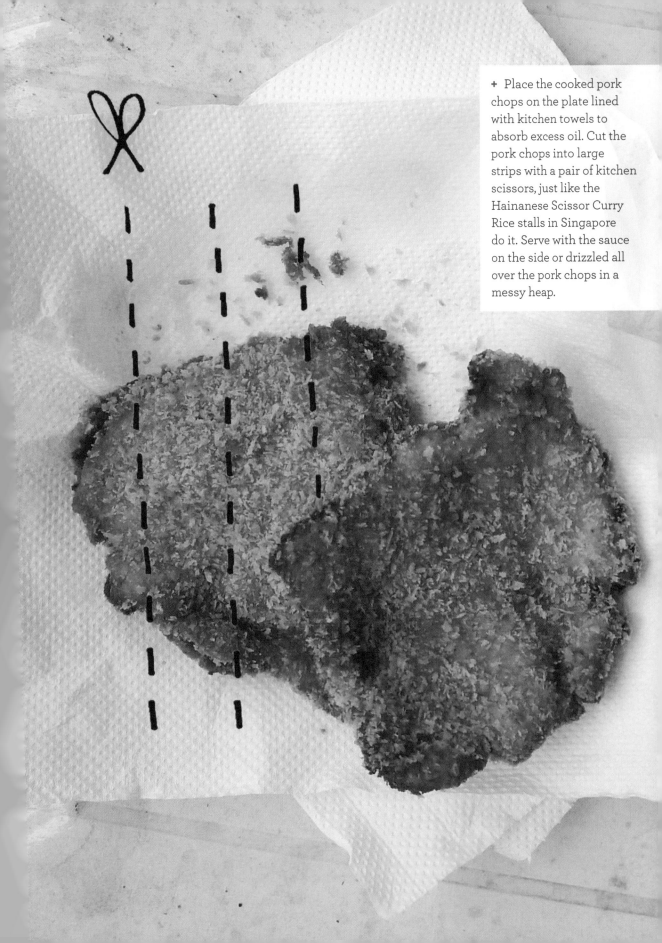

+ Place the cooked pork chops on the plate lined with kitchen towels to absorb excess oil. Cut the pork chops into large strips with a pair of kitchen scissors, just like the Hainanese Scissor Curry Rice stalls in Singapore do it. Serve with the sauce on the side or drizzled all over the pork chops in a messy heap.

WEN LIN: Ang Chow is a traditional Foochow delicacy made from fermenting glutinous rice for 30 days. The wine produced from this fermentation process, ang jiu, is used for cooking; it's a sweeter, more fragrant version of Shaoxing rice wine. If made well, the wine can be sipped like a dessert fortified wine. Practitioners of traditional Chinese medicine prescribe this wine to *por*, or 'mend' the health and strength of mothers who have just given birth. The red rice wine lees (ang chow) is an earthy, heady paste that can be used to cook many dishes. The signature dish is ang chow chicken with mee sua, a wheat-based vermicelli. Extended family in Indonesia tell me that they eat a quick-fermented version of ang chow as a topping on ice-cream! My mum also uses ang jiu and ang chow to cook pork and bamboo shoots, as well as chunks of shark. Both the wine and the lees can also be used to make ang chow pig's trotters.

ANG JIU AND ANG CHOW

Foochow Red Rice Wine and Wine Lees

MAKES 2–3 BOTTLES OF WINE AND 6–8 LARGE JARS OF WINE LEES

2 kg glutinous rice

½ cup water

5 pieces wine cake (jiu piah)

75 g red yeast rice (ang kek bee)

1 big glass or clay container with a cover

A NOTE ON WINE CAKES: These can be purchased from a Chinese medical hall or Chinese grocery. Broadly, there are two kinds of wine cakes you can use: sweet and 'hot', or what Western wine drinkers would understand as 'dry'. You can experiment with blends of both to get a flavour you like. My mum uses half of each type.

Before making the wine and wine lees, make sure your equipment and hands are absolutely clean. Just a few mould spores picked up with a speck of dirt will spread fast and cause mould to grow on your fermenting rice. If you happen to drop some rice on the floor, don't put it back in the container; throw it away.

STEAMING THE GLUTINOUS RICE—Wash the rice and soak it in water for at least 3 hours, or preferably overnight, making sure the rice is fully submerged. Drain and transfer to a baking tin that fits into your steaming device. Don't boil the rice in a rice cooker. Manually steaming the rice takes longer, but the longer exposure to steam means that more accidental bacteria on the rice will be killed. Use your fingers to poke holes all over the tray of levelled rice, and fill the tray with water so that the rice is half submerged, using the holes to gauge the level of water; the holes also help the rice to cook faster. Steam the rice for 30 minutes or until thoroughly cooked, stirring the rice several times throughout the steaming process. Loosen and spread the rice out to cool completely. This step is important as warm rice is the perfect breeding ground for mould, which can develop later as the rice is fermenting, so don't rush it.

PREPARING THE RICE FOR FERMENTATION—Boil ½ cup of water and let sit to cool. Blend the wine cakes and red yeast rice in a food processor or spice grinder. Transfer the resulting pink powder into a big bowl. Wet your hands in the cooled water. Take a fist-sized handful of the cooled rice and coat it with the pink powder. Transfer the powder-coated rice to a big glass or clay container. Repeat with the rest of the glutinous rice and powder until both are used up. Use the remaining boiled water to rinse any remaining rice or powder from the bowls into the large glass or clay container. ✦

+ FERMENTING THE RICE—Place the lid on the container, but do not tighten. Gases build up during the fermentation process so you'll need some way for the gases to escape, otherwise your whole container could explode and create a giant, bright-red horror movie mess. Set aside in a cool, dark place for 7 days.

On day 7, stir the mixture. Replace the cover loosely. Set aside for another 23 days; harvest the wine and wine lees on day 30. During the fermentation process, check on your glass container once a week.

HARVESTING THE WINE AND WINE LEES—The fermented mixture should have separated into two layers. The bulk of the residue, the wine lees, will be in the top layer. The bottom layer of liquid is the red rice wine. Strain the wetter wine lees by placing a sieve over a pot and straining until most of the wine drips through into the pot. Transfer the wine lees to glass jars.

CLARIFYING THE RICE WINE—Stick a funnel into a screw cap bottle and hold a muslin sieve (or coffee 'sock') above the funnel. Ladle the cloudy wine into the sock. The 'cloudy' residue collected in the sock has a slight perfumed, sweet taste and can be jarred separately and used to coat chicken before deep-frying it.

Cap the bottles of wine. The wine can be used for marinating meat and cooking. It will have more sweetness and fragrance than Shaoxing rice wine but when made well, it also tastes pretty good on its own! It's best consumed like a dessert wine, sipped in small quantities after a meal. Depending on the wine cakes you use and the length of ageing, the wine may taste light and fruity, then mature in flavour and taste more akin to a Chinese herbal wine.

WEN LIN: When plusixfive celebrated its one-year anniversary in London in June 2012, Goz decided to go with an all-pork theme and invited a whole bunch of us to cook with him. Our little collective of cooks did our best to use the lesser loved bits of pig (or lesser loved in London anyway). My Dad's Hakka side of the family is obsessed with pig's trotters. We cook up 3 giant pots from subtly different recipes every Chinese New Year. And even then, we sometimes run out and near-riots break out in my parents' living room. But I also wanted plusixfive's birthday party guests to try my mum's signature Foochow ang chow. So in an email from Singapore, my mum showed me how to combine my heritage from both sides of our family. Chef James Knappett, formerly of Marcus Wareing and The Ledbury, and a guest that day, hailed it as "bloody awesome".

ANG CHOW PIG'S TROTTERS

Hakka Pig's Trotters and Red Rice Wine Lees Stew

FEEDS 6–8

1.5–2 kg pig's trotters, chopped into large chunks

1 cup red rice wine (ang jiu) (page 148)

2 tsp sea salt

2 tsp sugar

2 tbsp vegetable oil

100 g ginger, smashed

5 cloves garlic, smashed with the skin on

1 cup water, boiling

10 tbsp red rice wine lees (ang chow) (page 148), plus additional to taste

Light soya sauce

Combine the pig's trotters, wine, salt and sugar in a Ziploc bag and let sit in the fridge overnight to marinate.

The next day, heat a large wok on high heat and add the oil. Fry the ginger and garlic for about 5 minutes. Add the wine lees and fry until fragrant. Stir fast to prevent burning, and lower the heat if needed. Add the trotters and stir until the wine lees are evenly spread. Add the liquid marinade from the Ziploc bag.

When the mixture comes to a boil, add the boiling water. Lower the heat and simmer for 1–2 hours until the trotters are soft and gelatinous (this depends on the breed of pig and the size of the trotter chunks). When the wine lees look dry, add a bit of water and stir to keep the bottom from burning. Add light soya sauce and extra wine to taste, then serve.

WEN LIN: Red rice wine is the key ingredient in the signature Foochow dish ang chow chicken mee sua soup, usually eaten on a birthday or a wedding because of its auspicious red colour.

ANG CHOW CHICKEN MEE SUA SOUP

Bloody Delicious Red Rice Wine Lees Chicken Soup with Vermicelli

FEEDS 6–8

1 large (1.5–2 kg) chicken,
   chopped into large pieces

1 cup red rice wine (ang jiu) (page 148)

2 tsp sea salt,
   plus additional for seasoning

2 tsp sugar

2 tbsp vegetable oil

100 g ginger, smashed

5 cloves garlic,
   smashed with the skin on

10 tbsp red rice wine lees (ang chow)
   (page 148)

1.5 litres unsalted chicken stock
   (page 46) or water

6–8 bundles mee sua
   (Chinese wheat vermicelli)

The day before serving, combine the chicken, wine, salt and sugar in a Ziploc bag and let sit in the fridge overnight to marinate.

The next day, drain the chicken and reserve the liquid marinade. Set both aside. Heat a large wok on high heat and add the oil. Fry the ginger and garlic for about 5 minutes. Add the wine lees and fry until fragrant, stirring fast to prevent burning. Lower the heat if needed. Transfer the chicken to the wok and stir until the wine lees are evenly combined. Transfer the liquid marinade to the wok.

Transfer the contents of the wok to a large stockpot. Add the chicken stock and bring to the boil. Lower the heat and simmer for 20–30 minutes, or until the chicken is cooked through. Add salt to taste.

Bring a small saucepan of water to a rolling boil. Using 1 bundle of mee sua per serving, boil the mee sua for a few minutes until soft. Drain and dish into individual bowls. Add the chicken and soup. Add salt and extra wine lees to taste, then serve.

MUM

My mum is ridiculously shy, which is why you don't see very many pictures of her in this book. In fact, when she sees this, I'll likely be subjected to weeks of nagging over the couple of photos I sneaked in here without her permission. But since she's the lady who taught me the basics of cooking, brought me up to be the human I am today, and who is generally responsible for giving me life over three decades ago, I thought it only apt to invite my mum to contribute her classic Hainanese chicken rice recipe to this book, a dish which she learnt from her own mother and which I ate a lot of when I was growing up.

My parents were working parents, so I spent a lot of time with my maternal grandparents as a wee little critter. My Hainanese grandmother, Ah Por, would often make this dish. Until today, every whiff of a steaming plate of chicken rice still brings me whizzing back to my grandparents' flat, bathed in the warm orange hue of the evening sun, and little me, pulling up my little plastic toy table and shovelling fluffy chicken rice into my fat face as I watched 6.30pm cartoons.

MUM: My daughter often tells me that the smell of chicken rice cooking in the kitchen is the quintessential smell of home. It's a dish I make often these days for special occasions. My mum used to make chicken rice for my brothers and me when we were growing up. For us siblings, it was always something we looked forward to, since our meals usually consisted of congee and fish.

My mum would steam the rice with lots of finely diced garlic and a bunch of fragrant pandan leaves, then she would compress the steamed rice into firm rice balls for us to eat. Not many people bother with making the rice balls any more—not even I do!

I remember my mum making chicken rice at a holiday chalet during a family vacation. I was helping her out in the kitchen, watching her prepare the ingredients, and—the all-important step—dipping the chicken in boiling water before covering the stockpot securely with the lid.

I remember her telling me it was crucial that no one open the stockpot lid before the chicken was ready, in order to preserve the heat. Soon after she'd told me this, in came my dad. He walked over to the stove and lifted the lid off the stockpot. Waves of precious steam escaped, much to the annoyance of my mum, who told him off in rapid Hainanese and shooed him out of the kitchen.

When my mum sent me her recipe, I wanted to publish it as is: a simple paragraph with no measurements, timings, or even ingredients. I realised that this was how I learnt to cook, through a lot of trial and error and a heck of a lot of experimentation. This was also how I gained my confidence in the kitchen, and more importantly, how I learnt to cook by tasting things along the way, fine-tuning until I made something I liked, not what some cookbook told me I ought to like. But my editor got anal and intervened, so here is my mum's recipe, demystified for all you lazy asses.

HAINANESE CHICKEN RICE

FEEDS 6

CHICKEN

1 kg whole chicken

Coarse sea salt

1 thumb-sized piece ginger, sliced

1 head garlic, crushed

2–3 pandan leaves, tied into a knot

Pinch of ground white pepper

Light soya sauce

Shaoxing rice wine

Sesame oil

SOUP

Half a white cabbage

Handful of ikan bilis (dried anchovies)

RICE

Good glug of rendered chicken fat
  or vegetable oil

3 cups jasmine rice

1 head garlic

1 knob ginger, finely chopped

Pinch of sea salt

Dash of light soya sauce

Dash of sesame oil

2–3 pandan leaves

+

TIP: To obtain chicken fat, ask your butcher for excess chicken skin and fat, they should give it to you for free.

To render chicken fat, fry the life out of it on medium heat. You should get a good amount which you can freeze for use in the future.

The night before serving, season the chicken by rubbing it all over with coarse sea salt. Stuff the chicken with the ginger, garlic, pandan leaves and pepper.

The next day, in a large pot, add enough water to cover the chicken and bring to a boil. Submerge the chicken in the water and boil for twenty minutes. Turn off the heat and leave the chicken to simmer for an hour. Drain and reserve the chicken stock to make the rice and soup. Let the chicken cool down, then rub all over with light soya sauce, rice wine and sesame oil.

To make the soup, add the cabbage and ikan bilis to the chicken stock and boil until the cabbage is cooked.

To make the rice, wash the uncooked rice and add the ginger, garlic, sea salt, light soya sauce, sesame oil, pandan leaves and rendered chicken fat. Use chicken stock in place of water and cook in a rice cooker or in a saucepan on the stove according to the instructions on page 48.

To make the chilli sauce, throw the chillies, garlic, ginger and lime juice in a blender. Slowly add the hot chicken stock and chicken fat as it blends. Season to your own tastes: add a dash of soya sauce and a teaspoon of sugar at a time and taste as you go along. If you want the sauce to be wetter, add more chicken stock. If you want it more sour, squeeze in more lime juice.

Chop the chicken into pieces and serve with a bowl of steaming hot rice and a bowl of chicken soup for the soul, accompanied by the chilli sauce, dark soya sauce and finely grated young ginger as side dips.

CHILLI SAUCE

8–10 fresh red chillies

2–4 red bird's eye chillies

1 head garlic

Small knob of young ginger

1 lime

Splash of rendered chicken fat

1 cup chicken stock (page 46),
    boiling hot

Light soya sauce

Sugar

OTHER CONDIMENTS

Thick dark soya sauce
    (chicken rice soya sauce)

Young ginger, finely grated

PA

In my growing-up years, my dad was always the super strict disciplinarian of the family, sternly trying to make sure I did everything right, from holding chopsticks properly (his greatest bugbear) to studying hard. So I never really conversed much with him as I was usually upset or angry with him, or, as was more often the case, him with me. I used to tell my much younger sis how she'd got it so easy because he used to be mighty strict and fierce with me but never with her (she puts it down to the fact that she is far cleverer and more obedient a child than I ever was—and she's probably right). To be fair to him, I did prefer Batman to biology, and would rather have been hanging out in Ngee Ann City, the largest shopping mall in town back then, trying to impress girls instead of doing my homework, while my Chinese-language education consisted mostly of reading Dragonball comics. But over the years though, Pa has really mellowed. In recent years, I've grown closer to my dad and so I was really pleased that he agreed to contribute to this cookbook.

One thing Pa has always been good at is creating things—every time there was a problem with some household appliance, he always had some fix for it. He was like a Singaporean MacGyver with a treasure trove of a storeroom filled with mysterious mechanical parts he would somehow fashion into something useful when needed. He probably got it from his own father, who was excellent at woodworking and made a couple of the furniture pieces that we still use daily. So it seems natural that with newfound time on his hands when he retired, he turned to cooking and recreating from memory the dishes that his mother used to make for him. The recipe that follows is one of those dishes.

PA: I grew up in a large family with five siblings, of whom I was the youngest. My own father was a strict disciplinarian with little time for lavishing care and attention on his children. This was probably because he had experienced the brutality of the Japanese Occupation, and worried constantly about his young family.

My mother, on the other hand, was kind and loving to all her children. She was also a fantastic cook who could always be depended upon to cook up a storm, even with my father's meagre income as a mechanic in an engineering workshop. Regardless of how hard times were, she would always ensure that we had something nice to eat. Even then, the need to stretch every cent meant that meat was a rare sight on the dining table. So having a chicken dish like kum jum gai for dinner was like manna from heaven.

PA: When properly marinated before steaming, the delicious fragrance of the coarse preserved turnip (chai poh), kum jum (golden needles or dried lily buds), sesame oil and ginger should permeate the tender slices of chicken. I still remember the wonderful smell wafting through our small and cramped flat. My mother would serve this dish topped with freshly chopped Chinese parsley. All of us siblings would crowd around the table, jostling for space and fighting over the gravy to spread on our rice.

KUM JUM GAI

Steamed Chicken with Rice Wine and Golden Needles

FEEDS 4–6

5 tbsp Shaoxing rice wine

4 tsp sesame oil

2 tbsp oyster sauce

1 tsp fish sauce

1 tbsp light soya sauce

2 tsp sugar

½ tsp ground white pepper

1 medium-sized chicken, jointed and chopped

20 g dried wood ear fungus, soaked in lukewarm water for 4 hours and thickly sliced

20 g dried shiitake mushrooms, soaked in lukewarm water for 4 hours and thinly sliced

30 g golden needles (dried lily buds), soaked in lukewarm water for 1 hour, hard ends trimmed off, and tied into a knot

20 g goji berries (gou qi zi)

10 g preserved turnip (chai poh), soaked in warm water for 10 minutes and coarsely chopped

Sea salt

In a large bowl, mix the rice wine, sesame oil, oyster sauce, fish sauce, light soya sauce, sugar and ground white pepper until well-combined. Add the chicken, ensuring that every piece is fully covered with marinade. Add the wood ear fungus, shiitake mushrooms, golden needles, goji berries and preserved turnip. Mix well. Let sit in the fridge to marinate for at least 4 hours.

Remove from the fridge and set aside until it reaches room temperature. Transfer the contents to a plate that fits your steaming appliance (I use a wok half-filled with water, and place a metal stand inside for the plate to rest on). Spread out the chicken, fungus and mushrooms to ensure they cook evenly. Let the water in your steamer come to a boil over high heat. Place the plate in the steamer, cover and steam for about 30 minutes, or until the chicken is cooked. To check for doneness, pierce the biggest piece of chicken with a knife. If the juices run clear, it's done. Season with salt to taste. Serve with steaming white rice.

TIP: For maximum flavour, use free-range, corn-fed chicken and young ginger. For added depth and flavour, stir in a spoonful of brandy before serving.

TYING LILY BUDS
FOR DUMMIES 1.

2.

3.

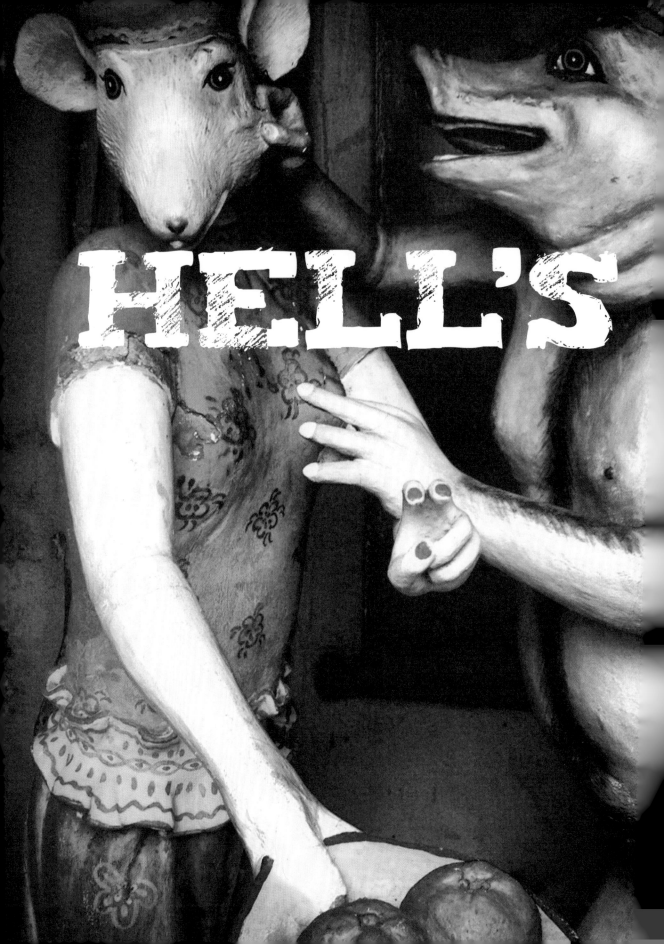

HELL'S

SALVATION

My earliest memory of eating the dish that follows comes from when I was about 12 years old. We had just visited Haw Par Villa, a Chinese mythology-themed amusement park. It was one weird place. Imagine if you put Ang Lee, David Lynch and Wes Craven in a room with a suitcase full of psychotropic drugs—this amusement park would be their demon lovechild. Haw Par Villa is a nightmare of weird and wonderful, fibreglass, technicoloured, weatherworn mannequins of Chinese monsters and demons grimacing and leering from behind bonsai trees and wispy willow plants at the odd Oriental damsel in distress and/or sexually ambiguous and disconcertingly young naked cherubs. The pièce de résistance however, was their star attraction, a water flume ride. It started off seemingly mundane as it went through the usual banal water splashes and lunges and dips. But just when I thought it was all over, the ride slowed down, forcing us through a dark, looming tunnel that showcased the 18 gates of Chinese hell in all their garish and grotesque glory.

So there I was, a fresh-faced and innocent 12-year-old, sitting in the flume ride, squealing with delight at the four-storey-tall slide, as I caught my breath and wiped the spray from my face, giggling in the afterglow. I sure as hell was not ready to be plunged into the belly of Hades, with little dioramas depicting scenes of thieves getting disembowelled, adulterers being castrated, liars getting their tongues seared off and just about everyone wailing as they were finished off in a flaming hot cauldron of oil, all under the watchful eyes of the gods of hell.

I still don't think I've fully recovered.

After surviving this traumatic experience, I remember my dad gleefully slapping me on the back, oblivious to the horrors his son had to endure, and bringing me shaking and shell-shocked to a little hole-in-the wall hawker stall selling braised duck. Indeed, hell's salvation is a dish of tender, juicy duck slow braised in a dark, deep, intensely spiced and fragrant soya sauce.

This dish can also be described as a soya sauce poached duck. The duck gently simmers in a spiced soya sauce and slowly absorbs the flavours of the aromatics; and because of the slow cooking process, retains its juicy tenderness. Always try to look for a fatty duck. A lean one is fine but it will not be as flavoursome. I also like to cook the duck whole, with the duck head and wing tips all on as these help impart more 'duckiness' to the soya sauce, which is later used as gravy. If you want the dish to be more substantial, add whole shiitake mushrooms and cubes of firm bean curd with the eggs.

LOR ARKH

Teochew Braised Duck

FEEDS 4–6

1 (1.5–2 kg) duck

Half a head of garlic, finely chopped; plus additional 20 cloves (leave the skins on if you're feeling lazy)

2 tsp sea salt, plus additional for seasoning

2 tsp ground white pepper, plus additional for seasoning

3 tbsp five-spice powder

Vegetable oil

5 star anise

5 cardamom pods

1 stick cinnamon

12 whole cloves

1 cup light brown sugar

8 tbsp dark soya sauce

3 tbsp light soya sauce

5 cups water

Sea salt

Ground white pepper

6 large eggs

1 tbsp cornflour, dissolved in 2 tbsp cold water

Sprig of coriander (cilantro), to garnish

TIPS: To carve or chop a duck: Place the duck on a chopping board. Find your heaviest knife. Remove the head and bishop's nose (aka its bum). Locate the joints of the duck and cut there (a process known as 'jointing'), to remove the thighs, front wings and drumsticks. Transfer these to a serving plate. The joints are the easiest and softest parts to cut through, otherwise you will be swearing a lot as you try to saw through the bones. Next, half the duck by chopping lengthwise through the soft ribcage. Then, slowly using the weight of the knife at even intervals, chop the duck crosswise into equal portions.

The night before serving, dry the duck with kitchen towels. Rub the skin and the inside of the cavity with half a head of garlic, 2 teaspoons of salt, 2 teaspoons of pepper and the five-spice powder, really rubbing it in to make sure that the flavours get absorbed. Let sit in the fridge, uncovered, overnight to marinate.

Remove the duck from the fridge and let sit until it reaches room temperature. In a pan wide enough to fit the whole duck, add oil to a depth of 1 cm and heat over high heat.

Add the duck, 20 cloves of garlic, star anise, cardamom, cinnamon and cloves to the pan. Fry the skin of the duck until it becomes brown and crispy and the spices become fragrant, about 10 minutes. Remove the duck and continue frying the spices for another 5 minutes until intensely fragrant. Set aside.

Transfer the duck to a large stockpot. Turn the heat to high and add the fragrant oil and spices, sugar, dark and light soya sauce and water. Make sure that the liquid gets into the cavity of the duck, as it will help to poach it. (Be careful, there's hot oil at work here!)

Bring to a rolling boil before reducing the heat. Simmer for 1½ hours, carefully and slowly turning the duck once after 45 minutes to ensure that the duck is coloured evenly. I usually use a pair of tongs for this as it can be quite tricky. Season with salt and white pepper to taste.

Turn off the heat, cover with a lid and leave the duck in the stockpot for another 30 minutes. Meanwhile, in another small pot, boil the eggs for 5 minutes. Remove and plunge the eggs into cold water to stop them from cooking. Peel and transfer the eggs to the stockpot to keep warm and absorb some colour and flavour from the poaching liquid. **+**

+ To make the gravy, transfer 3 cups of the poaching liquid to a small pot set over medium heat. Slowly drizzle in the cornflour solution to thicken the poaching liquid, stirring briskly to ensure there are no lumps. Add more water or poaching liquid depending on how salty you prefer it. Reduce the heat to low to keep warm.

To serve, remove the duck and let cool before chopping or carving. Halve or quarter the hardboiled eggs, then transfer to a serving plate with the duck and drizzle the gravy all over. Garnish with a sprig of coriander. Serve accompanied by a steaming plate of rice.

(MIS)
ADVENTURES

IN MOLECULAR GASTRONOMY

Before I toyed with the idea of starting a supper club, I was bitten by the molecular gastronomy bug. I bought all of Heston Blumenthal's books and watched all his TV shows religiously. I spent three days making his spaghetti bolognese, and before making his burgers, implored the butchers to lay the hand-ground beef in a particular manner "because Heston says so!" I was lucky enough to borrow a hopelessly expensive water circulator from Ben Greeno to sous-vide everything I could from Thomas Keller's *Under Pressure* (and in the process rack up a stupidly extortionate electricity bill). I even went so far as to write to an industrial food chemicals plant, National Starch and Chemical Co. in the UK, and managed to blag a free sample of tapioca maltodextrin, a compound that turns fat into powder, so I could make bacon powder and Nutella 'soil'.

So it seemed natural that when starting a Singaporean supper club came to mind, I thought, why bother just making good ol' Singaporean food? Why not jazz it up and make it molecular! Looking back with the power of 20/20 hindsight, I cringe that this thought even crossed my mind. After hours of sous-videing beef rendang, making weird agar noodles, and badgering an ex-girlfriend who was a doctor to bring me some syringes so I could inject pork chops with bak kut teh herbs and spices, I realised the concept just wasn't working.

One just shouldn't mess with generations of grannies and Peranakan aunties who've gotten it right. They sure as hell didn't have water circulators, alginates and water siphons. Hell, they didn't even have blenders back then—just a trusty old pestle and mortar, a well-worn wok, patience, and the wisdom to understand that good food comes to those who win the waiting game. The next recipe, beef rendang, celebrates the marriage of this waiting game and old-skool methods.

Although rendang resembles curry, it contains no curry spices. The closest I can get in English culinary terms would be a stew—a hearty, aromatic, melty coconut beef stew. I use ox cheek because it has tonnes of gelatinous properties and, when stewed for hours, breaks down and gives the rendang its rich creamy texture. Short ribs provide an intensely beefy flavour and retain their bite and shape even after hours of stewing. You can also use any stewing cuts like brisket.

BEEF RENDANG

Decadently Rich Ox Cheek and Short Rib Coconut Stew

FEEDS 6–8

50 g beef dripping (rendered according to the instructions for lard on page 44) or vegetable oil

1 stick cinnamon

5 whole cloves

4 star anise

4 cardamom pods

500 g ox cheek, chopped into 2.5-cm cubes

250 g beef short ribs, chopped into 2.5-cm cubes, reserving the bones

10 kaffir lime leaves, finely sliced

100 ml water

750 ml coconut milk

2 stalks lemongrass, white parts lightly bashed

4 tbsp tamarind pulp, seedless

150 g desiccated coconut, toasted (see page 43)

3 tbsp brown sugar or gula melaka (palm sugar)

2 tbsp dark soya sauce

2 tbsp light soya sauce

2 tbsp fish sauce

3 tbsp belacan (dried shrimp paste), shaved and toasted (see page 43)

Fresh red chillies, thinly sliced, to garnish

Fresh coriander leaves (cilantro), to garnish

+

TIP: This dish tastes way better the next day when all the flavours have had time to really sink in overnight and intensify.

To make the rempah, blend the garlic, onions, lemongrass, galangal, ginger and chillies in a food processor, or pound with a mortar and pestle until a smooth paste is formed. Add the 3 tablespoons of beef dripping a little at a time, to aid with the blending or pounding.

Heat the 50 g of beef dripping in a hot wok or a large ovenproof cast iron casserole until smoking hot. Add the rempah, cinnamon, cloves, star anise and cardamom. Stir constantly, ensuring it does not burn, for 15–20 minutes over medium heat, or until the rempah becomes intensely fragrant and takes on a dark brown hue.

Add the ox cheek, short ribs, beef bones and kaffir leaves and fry for another 15 minutes. Add the water, coconut milk, lemongrass, tamarind, desiccated coconut, sugar, dark soya sauce, light soya sauce, fish sauce and belacan, stirring constantly to ensure that it is well-mixed and every piece of beef is covered with the marinade.

Bring to a boil, then remove from the heat. Cover and put it in the oven at 150°C for 6 hours. Check on it every 2 hours, stirring to ensure that everything gets evenly exposed to the heat. If you notice that it is getting too dry, add 1 cup of water each time. Some people like a very dry beef rendang but I like mine to have the consistency of a thick, rich Irish stew. After 6 hours, remove the cover, turn the oven temperature up to 180°C and let the rendang get a searing blast of heat for 30 minutes.

Season according to taste. If you prefer it sweeter, add more sugar. If not spicy enough, add finely sliced dried chillies to the rendang while it's still hot, stirring them in. Leave the rendang to rest with the lid on for an hour before serving. To serve, remove the stalks of lemongrass and garnish with a sprinkling of sliced fresh red chillies and coriander leaves.

+

REMPAH (SPICE PASTE)

1 large head garlic, skinned

3 onions

5 stalks lemongrass

1 (10-cm) piece galangal

1 (5-cm) piece ginger

10 dried red chillies, soaked in
  lukewarm water for 1 hour,
  or red bird's eye chillies

3 tbsp beef dripping or
  vegetable oil

BEN

Ben Greeno has the dubious honour of being one of the reasons why this whole plusixfive supper club shindig started. So naturally, I was bloody thrilled (read: running in circles, arms flailing wildly, yelling OMGOMGOMG) when I got an email from him saying he was more than happy to contribute a recipe to this book, despite his ridiculously busy schedule as head chef of Momofuku Seiōbo.

BEN: I needed a break. After all, I had spent the last few years cooking and learning in some of the best, most intensive and inspiring kitchens in Europe and the US, including Sat Bains, Momofuku and Noma. What I soon learnt was that chefs don't know how to take it easy, so I started a supper club in London in 2010 called Tudor Road, with a focus on fresh, seasonal produce cooked like it has never been cooked before, showcasing locally foraged herbs and berries. It was also a good opportunity to stay sharp, to try and play with my own ideas.

More importantly, the supper club allowed me to meet the people I was cooking for, and to talk to a few people who enjoyed food for food's sake. It also allowed me to reach out to young people who wanted to go out and eat well without spending a fortune. They got to experience something just a little bit different, and that was what I wanted to achieve.

I met a lot of interesting people through Tudor Road, but Goz stood out. I always knew

the Chinese were madly enthusiastic about food, but this passionate guy embraced cooking and eating equally. We drank and chatted late into the night, and in the weeks to come, he would badger me for recipes and ideas, even hounding me for days to lend him my sous-vide water circulator until I finally relented.

He also convinced me to do a private supper club and set-up in his Islington flat, cooking for 14 of his friends. I guess it gave him the confidence that he could do the same, and it wasn't long before he set up plusixfive. One day, he invited me over for the very first trial session and I found myself eating, rather than cooking, in his flat. I felt proud and satisfied in equal measures to have inspired someone else to set up his own supper club and realise his dreams. It was wonderful to taste a truly honest, homely, thoughtful and heart-warming Singaporean dinner. The Tudor Road supper club, however, was short-lived, and it wasn't too long before the next big adventure came along and Momofuku Seiōbo was calling.

BEN: Since we embrace Asian flavours as part of our inspiration at Momofuku Seiōbo, it was easy to come up with something for Goz. This dish is relatively easy to make, delicious, and uses a part of the cow that is often neglected. Hope you like it.

WAGYU BEEF TONGUE, BLACK GARLIC, COURGETTE

'Ofally' Delicious

FEEDS 10

BRINE

1 wagyu beef tongue

2 litres water

20 g sugar

120 g sea salt

10 g pink salt

4 g coriander seeds

1 g black peppercorns

300 g black garlic

25 g sesame oil

200 g yogurt (the more acidic, the better), plus additional to garnish

1 yellow courgette (zucchini)

1 green courgette (zucchini)

Flake salt, for seasoning

Boil the ingredients for the brine for 30 minutes. Let sit in the fridge until cold, then add the tongue and let sit for another 24 hours in the fridge. An easier method for making brine if you do not have pots big enough is to freeze 1 litre of water in ice cube trays, then heat the remaining 1 litre of water with the brine ingredients, and combine the two.

Rinse the beef tongue. Place in a sealed bag and cook in a water bath at 68°C for 24 hours. The long and slow cooking process tenderises the proteins and breaks down the connective tissues.

Make the black garlic purée by blending the black garlic with water until smooth.

Blend the sesame oil with the yogurt. Cut the yellow courgettes into ribbons with a mandolin, ensuring that the ribbons are neither too thin nor too thick. Slice the green courgettes into thin disks.

When the tongue is cooked, let it cool, then peel the discoloured skin off with a vegetable peeler. Running it under cool water helps with the skinning process.

Thinly slice the tongue lengthwise. Number 2 on a meat slicer, if you have one. Otherwise use ninja knife skills.

Spread some garlic purée in the base of a bowl, top with some discs of courgette, then fold two slices of the tongue on top of that to give a 'wave effect'. Season with flake salt. Add the courgette ribbons on top of this and a few blobs of yogurt. Stick some shitty micro herbs on this if you like, but I wouldn't. Just eat.

SKIN AND BONES

I used to frequent a 12-seater, family-run Thai restaurant when I lived in King's Cross, London. It was a 'blink and you will miss it' hole-in-the-wall, run by a rotund, gap-toothed Thai granny. I always ordered the same thing there: deep-fried seabass with a grated papaya and green mango salsa topping. In Singapore, it is pretty de rigueur to consume the entire deep-fried fish—head, tail and all. Thai Granny would always beam with delight when she came to collect my spotless plate. She said it was so rare, and such a shame, that not many people enjoyed the fish head and tail.

At my favourite gastropub in London, The Eagle at Farringdon, where they sometimes serve whole grilled fish, the chefs told me that they often get the dish sent back with requests that the fish be topped and tailed. I've never understood that. The delicate meat on the fish head, especially the fish cheeks, is possibly the most delectable part of the fish. In larger fish, the gelatinous bits around the jaw and collar are so silky sweet, absorbing all the subtle flavours of the stock in which the fish was cooked.

One of the mottos behind plusixfive is to challenge what people think of food. So, to advertise a dinner where fish head curry was the main theme, I put up a gory picture of the fish head, mouth agape, with one eye staring out blankly and the other eye floating alongside, simmering in a pot of curry. Most of the time, however, I am pleasantly surprised by how game and adventurous my guests are—and none more so than those who signed up that day. We sold out in no time, and the guests mostly consisted of extremely curious and open-minded non-Orientals who were ready to be surprised and converted. At the end of the night, these fish-head converts even asked for seconds and takeaway packets. Thai Granny would've been proud.

Fish heads aren't always very meaty, so I sometimes add chunks of fish fillets to the curry. I like to add fairly robust fish such as skate or monkfish, which are not too delicate and won't disintegrate in the curry. Be careful when consuming this dish as there may be small, hard bones in the fish head that could be tough to spot in the curry, so you might want to warn your guests. You don't want them suing your ass off after half-choking to death at dinner. For the fish heads, ikan merah (red snapper) are traditionally used in Singapore, but I often find myself using salmon heads as they are easily obtained in London. The only problem with salmon is that they are very oily fish, so you need to occasionally skim the oil off the top of the curry.

ASSAM FISH HEAD CURRY

FEEDS 4

2 large fish heads

3 tbsp water, plus additional 1 cup

4 tbsp belacan (dried shrimp paste), toasted (see page 43)

100 g fish curry powder

3 tbsp tamarind pulp, seedless

8 large sweet ripe tomatoes, quartered

10 lady's fingers (okra), cut into 2.5-cm pieces

2 eggplant (aubergine), coarsely chopped into chunks

Handful of baby eggplant (aubergine) (optional)

3 tbsp fish sauce

2 tsp light soya sauce

Handful curry leaves, thinly sliced

Pinch of ground white pepper

440 ml coconut milk

3 tbsp brown sugar

Zest and juice from 5 limes

REMPAH (SPICE PASTE)

1 head garlic

10 red bird's eye chillies

5 large white onions

2 stalks lemongrass

1 (10-cm) piece galangal

3 tbsp vegetable oil

Wash the fish heads and remove the gills and innards. Chop the heads down the top into symmetrical halves and set aside.

To make the rempah, blend the garlic, bird's eye chillies, onions, lemongrass and galangal in a food processor, or pound with a mortar and pestle. Add the oil a little bit at a time to help with the blending or pounding until a smooth paste is formed.

Heat a large wok until hot, and fry the rempah over medium heat for 10–15 minutes. Stir constantly, making sure it does not burn. When the rempah is very fragrant and takes on a dark brown hue, add the 3 tablespoons of water, belacan and curry powder. Continue frying on high heat for 10 minutes.

Add the tamarind pulp and 1 cup of water to the wok and let it simmer gently over medium heat. Add the fish heads, vegetables, fish sauce, light soya sauce, curry leaves and ground white pepper. Stir to ensure that the fish and vegetables are all coated with the paste. Add the coconut milk, sugar and sufficient water to cover the fish heads.

Turn up the heat to high. When the curry has started to boil, reduce the heat to low. Add the lime juice and zest, and let the curry simmer gently for 2 hours. If it seems too watery, remove the lid and simmer over high heat, letting the curry slowly thicken.

Taste and add more lime juice or tamarind pulp if you prefer your curry more sour. Add more sugar if you prefer it sweeter.

ONCE UPON A TIME IN HONG KONG

Some time in late September 2012, I made the decision of moving to Hong Kong. I had found in Jason, Shu Han, Christine and others, a motley crew of crazed and amazing chefs whom I trusted to carry on the legacy of plusixfive in London, and felt that the time was right for me to leave. I would love to romanticise this and throw in a line here to say I moved because I wanted to expand the supper club internationally and realign the skewed misconceptions of Singaporean food, striking at the heart of the country that invented the diabolical Singaporean fried noodles... but, alas, the truth could not be more bland—I moved because my day job gave me the opportunity to relocate and assist in the set-up of our Hong Kong office.

I did toy with the idea of starting a supper club in Hong Kong. I had heard that the supper club scene in Hong Kong was vastly different from the one in London. Although many of the supper clubs (or private dining, as they are called) were housed in residential buildings or warehouses, upon entry, more often than not, you would be greeted with table service, linen and sometimes even waiters. They were basically full-fledged restaurants run out of residential settings and didn't have the charming, rough-and-ready, feasting-at-a-mate's-house feel which most of the London supper clubs had. This spurred me on however, and I had lofty dreams of how I was going to change this and hopefully bring the plusixfive experience to people in Hong Kong.

But that lofty dream of a supper club remained just that—a mere dream. Upon entry into the service apartment where I was being housed, I was struck dumb by the reality of how teeny apartments in Hong Kong were.

There was one A3-sized ledge that doubled as a bar counter, and which I assumed also served as the 'dining table'. Underneath that, if you carefully shimmied the single bar stool to one side (carefully because you had nowhere else to put your groceries, so you had to place them on the stool), you could access the fridge which was so embarrassingly small, it made hotel minibars look cavernous. Adjacent to the aeroplane toilet-sized sink was a workspace on which a Christmas card-sized chopping board sat snugly. To the right were two small electric stoves which were so close to each other that the one pot which came with the apartment had to sit astride them both—presumably for efficient boiling purposes, or as some sort of sick in-joke between the owners of the building. There were empty salt and pepper shakers, a number of rudimentary eating utensils and a knife so blunt, it was tofu-resistant. Oh, there were also a dozen wine glasses, a dozen champagne glasses,

But that lofty dream of a supper club remained just that—a mere dream. Upon entry into the service apartment where I was being housed, I was struck dumb by the reality of how teeny apartments in Hong Kong were.

I can only
assume that
the owners of
this service
apartment
thought all
expats in Hong
Kong lived like
P Diddy, throwing
obscenely
resplendent
parties and
having Cristal
showers
every night.

a dozen martini glasses, a cocktail shaker, a cocktail-making set, a champagne bucket, and four bottle openers. I can only assume that the owners of this service apartment thought all expats in Hong Kong lived like P Diddy, throwing obscenely resplendent parties and having Cristal showers every night. Cooking, of course, had no place in the lives of young, hot-blooded expats who lived only on a steady diet of cigarettes and alcohol. So as I closed the door of the fragile cabinet filled with useless stemware, I also slammed shut any notions of opening a supper club in Hong Kong.

Perhaps I was displaying all the classic tell-tale signs of plusixfive withdrawal—cold sweat, anxiety, chills of jealous pangs whenever I saw pots, pans and other seemingly innocuous kitchen utensils, eyes distractedly darting back and forth whenever I saw a potential location for a possible plusixfive pop-up event—but when I met up with Charmaine, who used to be a food writer for *Time Out London*, she immediately mooted the idea of hosting something in Hong Kong. The culinary equivalent of a human Facebook, this girl had connections everywhere for all things food-related in Hong Kong. After a flurry of emails, WhatsApp messages and brainstorming cocktail sessions, I managed to secure a slot at Island East Markets, a new farmers' market and the brainchild of the multi-talented Janice of e-tingfood.com.

And with that, plusixfive 小牌檔 was born.

After the initial elation of securing a slot at this farmers' market wore off like a bad acid trip, the harsh reality of what was to come set in. I'm still not sure how I managed to prep a hundred servings of beef rendang, chwee kueh or laksa in that toy-sized kitchen of mine. Or how Charmaine kneaded, proofed and churned out over 60 mantou buns from her teeny kitchen using a variety of miniature, makeshift steaming appliances. Or how we were the first stall to sell out, pack up and go home in less than four hours despite the torrential rainfall. But everything just came together so poetically in the end. I guess there is a heck of a lot of truth in what ol' Abe Lincoln said: "Determine that the thing can and shall be done, and then we shall find the way."

CHARMAINE

Charmaine (or SuperCharz as she is known in real life) is a brilliant, lyrical food writer who used to work for *Time Out London* and a variety of other publications, but more importantly, she is one exuberant, charming, smiley, spritely little bubble of ideas. She had been to a couple of my supper clubs in London and had heard about my relocation to Hong Kong, where she was now living. We forged a largely food-based friendship over Twitter in the months before she left London. In Hong Kong, she somehow managed to ply me with food and drink until she'd convinced me to continue the legacy of plusixfive in Hong Kong—beginning with our first pop-up stall, plusixfive 小牌檔.

CHARMAINE: From the moment Goz let me have a go on his ice shaver, I knew we would be good friends for life. Yeah G! During his stint in Hong Kong we managed to rock Island East Markets (to the tune of Beastie Boys, natch) along with Goz's awesome fiancée, Phoebe, and Tupperware champion, Andrew. It rained, it poured, and the pot holding the precious laksa elixir would not stop jiggling (much like us). Yet we all came together to show Hong Kong proper plusixfive cooking. All those nights of chinwagging and plotting in speakeasies and scheming on the pavement of Shanghai Street were worth it—how incredible it is to imagine Goz's magic stretching from a northeast London flat to an urban farmers' market in Hong Kong. Here's to taking over the world!

The following recipe comes from my dad Erwin, nicknamed 3B (pronounced 'saam bee') because he was the third baby in his family.

Stuck in the middle, with two brothers and two sisters, it seemed only natural for him to always try and stand out. For as long as I can remember, his cooking has always included some sort of Mad Hatter twist.

My dad has always been crazy good at using whatever is lying around the house to solve problems; not out of frugality, but because he just likes figuring out how to do things in his own creative way. This recipe is a testament to his carefree, but always delicious, way in the kitchen, where rules are meant to be broken. Tea-smoked poultry is a common enough dish, but typically, 3B asks, why stick with just tea when there's SO MUCH STUFF here my lazy daughter buys but never gets around to using? So this recipe is also inadvertently a homage to the crazy supper club way of life—put together a load of random shiz (read: people) and magic happens. Or maybe I'm just saying plusixfive is smokin'.

CHARMAINE: When I asked my dad to share this recipe, we embarked on a mini foraging trip around our tiny Hong Kong flat to find things to flavour our chook with: old coffee grounds from Ho Chi Minh City (not good enough to brew, but still fragrant enough to cook with), fresh kumquat leaves from the pot on the windowsill, dried chillies and lime leaves from my curry-making phase a few months before. He also revealed his stash of dried shiitake mushroom stems—usually tossed away by chefs after the caps are used, he keeps them to add little dashes of umami to dishes. Nothing goes to waste in his kitchen. And my mum and I are always the happy guinea pigs.

'WHATEVER YOU HAVE' SMOKED SOYA SAUCE CHICKEN

FEEDS 2–3

SOYA SAUCE MARINADE

250 ml dark soya sauce

125 ml light soya sauce

900 ml water

1 large piece rock sugar

2 star anise

1 (2.5 by 2.5-cm) dried mandarin peel

1 tsp Sichuan peppercorns

1 (2.5 by 5-cm) piece fresh ginger, sliced

4 cloves garlic, peeled and crushed

4 stalks spring onions, thinly sliced

50 ml Shaoxing rice wine

CHICKEN

1 heaped tbsp sea salt

Half a small chicken, skin on

1 tsp five-spice salt

2 tbsp dark rum

1 tsp runny honey

+

Add all the ingredients for the marinade into a pot large enough to fit the chicken. Bring to the boil, then reduce to a simmer. Cook for 10–15 minutes, then remove the pot from the heat and set aside.

To make the chicken, add the sea salt to a large pot of water and bring to the boil. Once boiling, blanch the chicken to remove any blood and impurities, then drain and plunge the chicken in cold water to rinse.

Bring the marinade back to the boil and add the chicken, breast-side down. Cook for 15 minutes, turning once or twice, then cover with a tight-fitting lid and turn off the heat. The residual heat will continue to cook the chicken, which should be around 80 per cent done in 20 minutes, depending on the size of the bird. You don't want it to be completely cooked as it will be smoked as well. Leave the chicken to marinate in the sauce.

Line an old wok with aluminium foil and add all the 'smoke' ingredients, mixing them well. Place a metal rack over the ingredients, cover the wok with a tight-fitting lid and heat over high heat until the brown candy sugar begins to melt and caramelise. Reduce the heat once the mixture starts to smoke— you don't want it to burn!

Remove the chicken from the marinade—it should be nice and burnished brown by now—and season the underside with some five spice salt. Place the chicken on the rack, cover the wok and smoke for 10 minutes.

Turn the chicken over and sprinkle on a bit more five spice salt. Smoke for another 10 minutes. Mix the dark rum and honey, then brush over the chicken during the last 5 minutes of smoking. ++

SMOKIN' LEGS

darling...

+

FOR THE 'SMOKE'

1 handful cooked rice, preferably
   left over from the day before

1 small handful uncooked
   white rice

2–3 tbsp oats

12 dried shiitake mushroom
   stems

2 tbsp green tea leaves

2 tbsp black tea leaves

1–2 tbsp finely ground coffee

1 (2.5 by 2.5-cm) fresh orange
   peel, torn into pieces

1 rectangular slab
   Chinese brown candy sugar
   (peen tong), chopped

1 small dried red chilli

1–2 fragrant leaves,
   such as kaffir or kumquat

2–3 tbsp Shaoxing rice wine
   or dry white wine

++ Check for doneness
by piercing the chicken at
its thickest part, near the
top of the thigh. If it's
cooked, the juices should
run clear. Chop into pieces
with a cleaver—like a
badass Chinese butcher—
and serve, preferably
accompanied by lots of
steamed, fluffy white rice
and simple, fresh green
vegetables.

MATT

Whenever a friend visits me in Hong Kong, I bring them to Yardbird. Whenever I'm meeting a friend and we're stumped for ideas, I suggest Yardbird. And whenever I'm asked for a restaurant recommendation, the first name to roll off my tongue is Yardbird. When I first moved to Hong Kong, one of the first places my friend Charmaine brought me to was this little izakaya. By happy coincidence, I realised it was located just five-minutes' walk from my service apartment, so it became the de facto place where I could be found every other week. I love everything about the restaurant, from the minimalist lines and the extremely energetic and lively service crew to the fact that chef Matt uses fresh, locally sourced, natural ingredients whenever possible. All their chickens are from the New Territories and they have no proper freezer facility, which means everything is brought in fresh every single day. So you can't imagine my insane delight (fist-punching-air-silly-victory-dance) when Matt agreed to contribute the recipe for their most iconic and famous dish: the Yardbird meatball.

MATT: My passion for food and art has taken me on travels throughout Asia, where I was able to explore different food cultures. While travelling in Japan, I fell in love with the interplay of food, art and craftsmanship. Both my father and grandfather worked as carpenters, and I've always felt that quality of material is just as important as the manner in which that material is treated; this is the underlying philosophy of Japanese cuisine and the reason why I fell in love with it.

The first formal Japanese kitchen I worked at was in Vancouver, at a restaurant called Shiru-Bay Chopstick Café. As the only non-Japanese chef there, the learning curve was steep; however, the exposure to the simple art of Japanese cooking confirmed my passion for the cuisine. After establishing myself at Shiru-Bay, I was approached by a group of regular customers who were in the process of opening their own restaurant, Ch'i,

where I later became executive chef.

Once I felt that I had learned everything I could at Ch'i, I moved to New York City to expand my culinary education. It was at Masa that I found a great mentor and teacher in 'Taisho', Masayoshi Takayama. I spent three years under Takayama's direct instruction and guidance, an apprenticeship that allowed me to develop strong skills and that, essentially, made me the chef I am today.

I moved to Hong Kong in 2009, where the food culture inspired me to pursue my lifelong dream of opening my own restaurant, and after two years as executive chef of Zuma, I finally decided to do it. With business partner Lindsay Jang, I opened my first restaurant, Yardbird, in the Sheung Wan district of Hong Kong. Inspired by the yakitori-ya restaurants of Japan, Yardbird specialises in yakitori dishes of skewered grilled chicken.

MATT: It is said that a yakitori restaurant can be judged by its tsukune, or meatball, so at Yardbird we tried endless combinations. We figured out that the part of the chicken that gave us the best ratio of fat to meat was the drumstick of the wing. In addition to this, you'll have to ask your butcher in advance for the soft breast-bone cartilage found in between the breast of a chicken; it takes quite a few chickens to reach a substantial amount of meat, so preparing in advance is key. Another important component of the tsukune is the egg yolk that has been marinated in our tare sauce. The eggs are still essentially raw so it's very important to buy the highest quality eggs that you can find. Tare is essentially teriyaki sauce that has been fortified with chicken bones, and every yakitori restaurant has their own flavour of tare. The Yardbird tare sauce is fairly balanced—slightly sweet, with ginger, spring onion and a strong chicken flavour.

MEATBALL + EGG YOLK, TARE SAUCE

MAKES ABOUT 4 JARS OF SAUCE AND 40–50 SKEWERS

YARDBIRD TARE SAUCE

900 ml sake

750 ml mirin

250 g Tokyo onions or spring onions, white stems removed

100 g ginger

1 kg chicken bones

500 ml Japanese soya sauce

500 g zarame sugar or any granulated brown sugar

300 ml tamari soya sauce

MEATBALL

1.5 kg chicken wing drumstick meat

350 g chicken breastbone cartilage

15 g sea salt

300 g white onion, thoroughly washed, finely chopped and squeezed dry

1 g freshly ground black pepper

120 g panko breadcrumbs

Tare sauce

High-quality egg yolks (one per skewer per serving)

To make the tare sauce, burn off the alcohol from the sake and mirin (be careful as this will flame up pretty high). Preheat the barbecue or the oven on its grill setting at medium heat. Using the Tokyo onion tops and ginger as a bed for the chicken bones, splash everything with some of the sake and broil until the bones are dark golden brown and the onions are thoroughly wilted. Drain any fat that is left over and set aside. Heat the sake and mirin over low heat. Add the sugar and mix until completely dissolved. Add the bones, ginger and onions. Continue to cook over low heat for 10 minutes, then add the Japanese soya sauce and tamari soya sauce. Cook on the gentlest simmer for about 1½ hours. Be careful not to boil rapidly as the soya sauce will burn, which will lead to a bitter-tasting sauce. Skim off any fat and strain well. The sauce keeps very well refrigerated.

Carefully remove the meat from the drumstick portion of the chicken wings, including the skin and small bits of cartilage, but not the bone. Place the meat on a tray and freeze for 20–30 minutes, along with the mechanisms of a meat grinder. Dice the soft breastbone as finely as you can. Remove the drumstick meat from the freezer and grind immediately. Put the drumstick meat back through the grinder again. Vigorously mix in the soft breastbone and salt by hand until the mixture becomes dense. Add the onions, breadcrumbs and pepper. Portion the meatball mixture into 50 g balls. Poke a 15-cm bamboo skewer through each ball, and keep refrigerated.

When the oven is ready, grill the skewers slowly over the barbecue or in the oven until golden brown.

Dilute the tare sauce with equal parts room-temperature water, then carefully add the egg yolks and let sit in the refrigerator for 2 hours. Place each semi-cured egg yolk into a small bowl and add 1–2 tablespoons of tare sauce. We encourage our guests to mix the egg yolk vigorously in the tare sauce and dip the meatball skewer inside.

ONE NIGHT WITH LADY LAKSA

The recipe that follows is a Frankenstein's monster, loosely based on a recipe by Jason and modified by me, incorporating what I'd learnt at one of Singapore's oldest and largest karaoke nightclubs. Yes, you heard that right, a karaoke nightclub—where middle-aged businessmen slip into the wee hours of the night with wine, women and song.

The unlikely story, as always, begins with food. Over dinner with some friends in London, they started singing the praises of the laksa at a well-known and preeminent nightclub in Singapore. Since none of them seemed to fit the archetypal clientele, I asked how they knew and more importantly, why the hell they went to the most unexpected of places to eat a bowl of curry noodle soup. It turned out that the father of my Singaporean friend B ran the place and B always organised parties there for her friends. Laksa, which was a regular staff meal item cooked in the nightclub's kitchen, was almost always served at these parties.

B kindly arranged for me to sneak into the kitchens of her father's establishment and I found myself under the tutelage of the very bemused Ah Suan, the resident chef who has been with the nightclub for more than 20 years, learning how to make her legendary laksa.

This was one of the three dishes that was served at plusixfive 小牌檔, and if the sales on that rainy day we debuted in Hong Kong are anything to go by, there truly is nothing more comforting on a cold, wet day then a bowl of hot, rich laksa.

There are two things I cannot stress enough about this dish. One is the noodles, which can be hard to find outside Singapore and Malaysia. In London's Chinatown, you can find the thoughtfully named and conveniently pre-packed dried 'Singapore Laksa Noodles'. It's thicker than regular vermicelli, but thinner than Japanese udon. The other crucial ingredient is laksa leaves (daun kesom), which provides laksa's quintessential fragrance and is sprinkled on right before serving. It can be found in most Vietnamese supermarkets. Lastly, you can substitute any good chicken or seafood stock, though it won't be as rich and flavoursome.

LAKSA

Noodles in Rich Creamy Curry Coconut Broth

FEEDS 4

700 ml Stock of Ages (page 46)

100 ml water

100 g ikan bilis (dried anchovies)

4 tbsp vegetable oil

1.4 litres coconut milk

Fish sauce

Sugar

Sea salt

REMPAH (SPICE PASTE)

12–15 large dried red chillies, soaked in lukewarm water for 1 hour

200 g dried shrimp (hae bee), soaked in lukewarm water for 4 hours

2 stalks lemongrass, sliced thinly

1 (4-cm) cube belacan (dried shrimp paste), toasted (see page 43)

10 candlenuts or macadamia nuts

1 (5-cm) piece fresh galangal, skinned and chopped

8 shallots, chopped

1 head garlic, crushed

1 tbsp coriander seeds

2 tbsp ground turmeric

2 tbsp sambal tumis belacan (page 118)

4 tbsp vegetable oil

+

In a large stockpot, boil up the Stock of Ages and water. Add the ikan bilis and let it slowly simmer for 1 hour on medium heat, then reduce the heat to low and gently simmer.

Meanwhile, blend all the ingredients for the rempah in a food processor or pound with a mortar and pestle until a smooth paste is formed.

Heat 4 tablespoons of vegetable oil in a pan over medium heat and fry the rempah for 10–15 minutes, or until dark brown and intensely fragrant. Add the rempah and coconut milk to the stockpot and bring to a rolling boil over high heat. Season with fish sauce, sugar and salt to taste.

Cook the noodles according to the manufacturer's instructions.

To serve, divide the noodles into four bowls. Garnish with tau pok, fishcakes, prawns, a clump of Meat Shreds, eggs and bean sprouts. Ladle in the broth, add a sprinkling of laksa leaves and serve with dollops of sambal tumis belacan.

TO SERVE

300 g dried thick rice
vermicelli (thick bee hoon),
cooked according to
manufacturer's instructions

12 pieces tau pok
(fried bean curd), halved

Pan-fried Chinese fishcakes,
sliced (however many you
want per person)

Tiger prawns, cooked

200 g Meat Shreds (page 46)
(optional)

4 eggs, hard-boiled and halved

Large handful of bean sprouts,
tailed and lightly blanched

Small handful of laksa leaves
(daun kesom), finely chopped

Sambal tumis belacan
(page 118)

SHIOK !!!

GRACE

Grace is a dear frenemy of mine. She is like the (marginally) older sister I never had. We both have the most irreverent, rib-tickling sense of humour, but we also have pretty intense squabbles over some of the most meaningless things. Nothing gives me more pleasure than to irritate the shit out of her. I can safely say she probably feels the same way about me too. One thing about Grace though, is that you can always count on her for a helping hand. So when plusixfive's popularity outgrew the one table I had, she loaned me a spare collapsible table she wasn't using. This table (and Grace's constant harping on how she has indirectly contributed to the successes of plusixfive) has been a mainstay of the supper club ever since.

GRACE: I always knew that Goz's incredible passion for all things edible would translate into something more than the occasional dinner party for friends. He still does the quintessential dinner party with panache and flair, but his journey with food has certainly evolved far beyond.

As a friend who has benefitted largely from the food off his table, I was eager to take part in this exciting new adventure, although I have to confess that my intentions were not altogether altruistic. I am glad to report that one year on, my tummy is still happily satisfied.

Many people were a part of this process from conception to fruition but I suppose my biggest contribution was a foldable table from Argos.

Goz needed furniture in his apartment that would suit the demands of having 20 guests, yet could be stowed away when not in use. We had 24 hours to find a table, and I had one, which I gladly 'loaned'. This table is symbolic, for it has borne witness to plusixfive's incredible journey. It graced the first supper club and still sits in the home of plusixfive today, bearing the weight of the delightful offerings the supper club continues to offer. It is probably safe to say that I will not be getting the table back and so my connection to plusixfive continues to endure. It is in this capacity as one-time owner of this crucial table that I contribute my favourite recipe for char kway teow.

GRACE: In Singapore, it is easy to dismiss this flat rice noodle dish as common. After all, why bother getting yourself hot and bothered when the uncle at the hawker centre can deliver this steaming plate of deliciousness without any fuss? What most people don't know is that char kway teow is also easy and inexpensive to make yourself. A great way to feed guests well without forking out a king's ransom, it can also be quickly and efficiently put together for single diners. It's cheap, cheerful and tasty! You don't have to de-vein the prawns if you don't mind eating the defecation of a crustacean. Personally, I do mind, so I always buy them de-veined or alternatively, persuade my husband to 'do me a favour'.

CHAR KWAY TEOW

Messy Oily Sweet Fried Noodles

FEEDS 2
(OR 1 WITH A BIG HEARTY APPETITE)

250 g kway teow (flat rice noodles)

2 fresh red chillies, more if you prefer it spicier

2 cloves garlic

4 shallots

2 tbsp vegetable oil

50 g prawns, shelled and de-veined

1 cup bean sprouts, tailed

1 stalk chye sim (flowering Chinese cabbage), cut into 3-cm pieces

2 tsp light soya sauce

1 egg, beaten

1 tbsp dark soya sauce

1 tbsp kecap manis (sweet soya sauce) (optional)

Wash the kway teow and drain well. To make the rempah (spice paste), blend the chillies, garlic and shallots in a food processor, or pound with a mortar and pestle until a smooth paste is formed. Heat the oil in a wok or large frying pan over high heat. When the oil is hot, fry the rempah for 2–3 minutes, or until fragrant.

Add the kway teow noodles and fry well for 5 minutes. Add the prawns, bean sprouts, chye sim, light soya sauce and dark soya sauce. Mix well and fry for another 5 minutes, or until the vegetables are cooked.

Make a well in the middle and add the beaten egg, stirring slowly until the egg is cooked. Then mix in with the rest of the ingredients.

If you want the dish to be slightly sweet, add the kecap manis at this stage. Remove from the heat and serve steaming hot.

BONUS: Chinese sausages (lap cheong) make an awesome addition to this dish if you can seek out some of good quality. Thinly slice one or two and add with the prawns and vegetables.

If your lucky stars are aligned and you can get your paws on them, I also love to chuck in a handful of blanched blood cockles along with the prawns. The sharp, iron-y, bloody taste provides a refreshing zing that cuts through the richness of the dish.

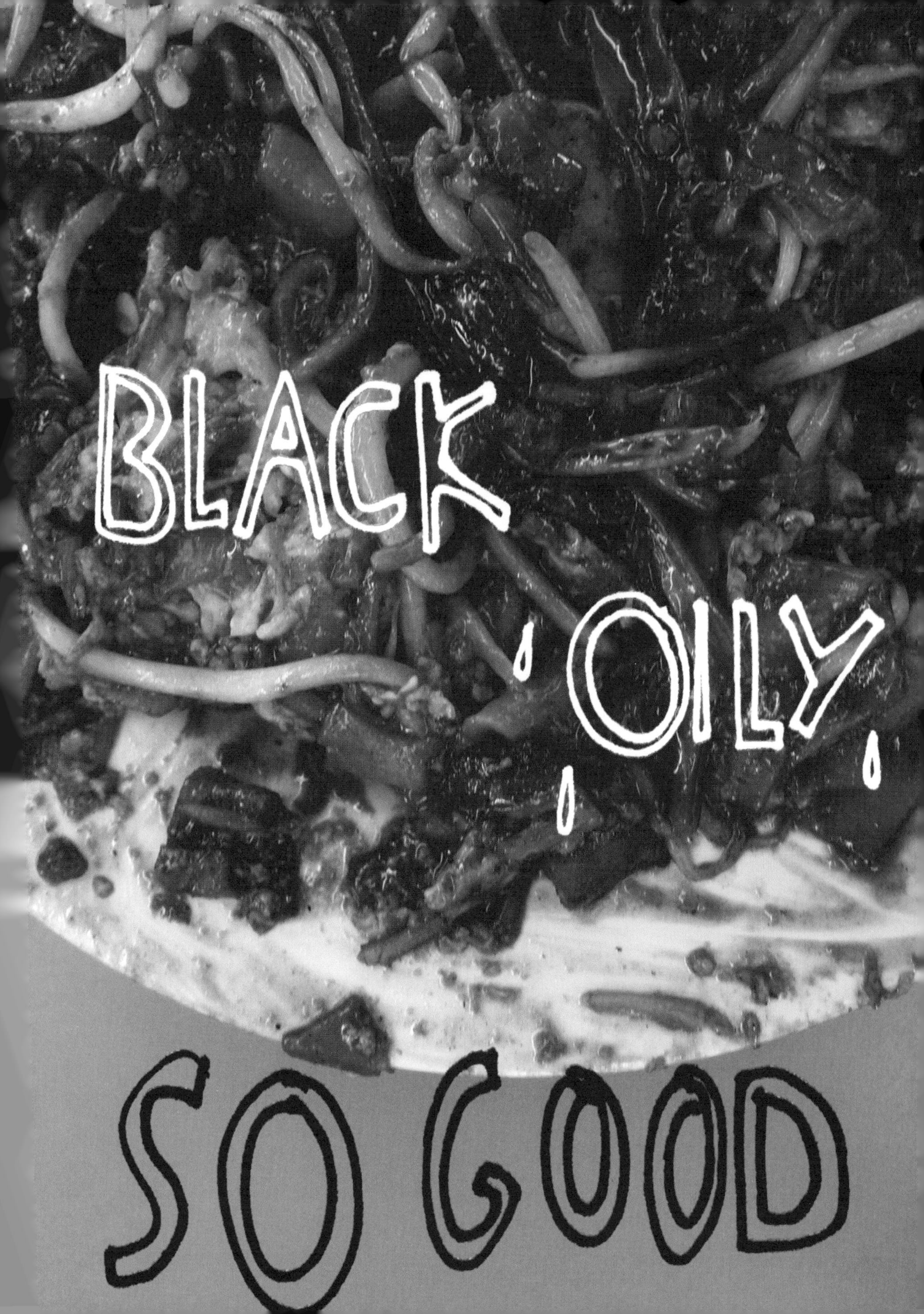
BLACK
OILY
SO GOOD

DON'T JUNK THE SPAM

My friend Weiyi once told me the story of how Singapore fried noodles was invented. Like most Hainanese men who came over to Singapore, her grandfather was a chef on a British naval ship. Late into the night, sailors would often get hungry and ask for supper. Not wanting to use the next day's rations, the chefs would fumble around looking for leftovers in the kitchen larder and rummage up whatever they could find, frying it up with noodles. The penchant for this late night snack then spread to the UK and the rest of the British Empire—in particular Hong Kong, where this dish is now as ubiquitous as Vegemite in Australia.

Whatever its origins, this luminous yellow fried noodle dish is probably as familiar to a regular Singaporean as a freezer is to an Inuit. That said, we do commonly eat fried bee hoon, or vermicelli noodles, for breakfast— a real breakfast of champions. These breakfast noodles are wok-fried in lard, with an unhealthy serving of deep-fried comestibles, from chicken wings and fish balls to fish cakes and semi-runny sunny-side ups with white edges so crispy, they could only be achieved by, yes, deep frying.

And of course, there's the deep-fried luncheon meat, or Spam. Most people in the West seem to instinctively hate it, recoiling with scrunched up faces at the merest whisper of the word—but in Hong Kong, every other dish in a *cha chan teng*, the fragrant harbour's version of an American diner, has the option to add luncheon meat, especially at breakfast. Yes, it's bright pink and canned and the animal probably died 20 years before you opened the tin, but hey, I cannot think of anything more visceral and primal than sinking your teeth into a deep-fried luncheon meat sandwich as the oil oozes down your fingers. Pure bliss. So yes, don't forget the luncheon meat, OK?

The key to this dish is a good stock. If you do not have the time to make the Stock of Ages, use a good chicken or pork stock. The lard also plays an important part in the dish, as does the soaking liquid. If you can find flat rice noodles (kway teow), you may wish to substitute some of the dried rice vermicelli (bee hoon) for this as well to give it a different texture. Be very careful not to overcook the noodles. Cooking the noodles should not take very long, probably 3–5 minutes, depending on how high the temperature of your stove goes. There is nothing worse then soft, mushy noodles broken into teeny pieces—unless you are a toothless, gummy geriatric.

SINGAPORE BREAKFAST FRIED NOODLES

No. Not That Kind of Singapore Fried Noodles

FEEDS 4–6

400 g dried rice vermicelli (bee hoon)

Stock of Ages (page 46),
  for boiling noodles

5 tbsp lard (page 44) or vegetable oil

1 tbsp sesame oil

20 shallots, finely chopped

2 heads garlic, finely choped

1 (10-cm) piece ginger, thinly sliced

100 g dried shrimp (hae bee), soaked in
  lukewarm water for 4 hours, reserving
  the soaking liquid

300 g pork belly, thinly sliced

1 white cabbage, thinly sliced

200 g shiitake mushrooms, thinly sliced,
  (If using dried mushrooms, soak for
  4 hours, reserving the soaking liquid.)

6 tsp fish sauce

5 tsp oyster sauce

5 tsp dark soya sauce

Pinch of ground white pepper

Sea salt

Fried shallots (page 39), to garnish

Crackling from rendered lard
  (page 44), to garnish

Sliced pickled green chillies, to garnish

Fresh red chillies, thinly sliced,
  to garnish

Sambal tumis belacan (page 118),
  to garnish

Accompaniments such as pan-fried
  prawns, fishcakes, luncheon meat,
  sunny-side-up eggs, deep-fried
  chicken wings, or as desired

Submerge the dried rice vermicelli in cold water for about 1½ hours. It should reconstitute into a tangle of noodles but still be quite hard. In a small pot, add enough room-temperature Stock of Ages to submerge the vermicelli. Add the vermicelli and soak for another 30 minutes. The vermicelli should be on the harder side of al dente at this point. Remove from the stock and set aside.

In a wok or large pan, heat the lard and sesame oil on high heat until it's smoking hot. If adding accompaniments to your noodles, you can take this opportunity to fry them in the scalding fat. Reduce the heat to medium. Add the shallots, garlic, ginger and dried shrimp. Fry until fragrant. Add the pork belly, cabbage and mushrooms, and stir-fry for 5 minutes.

Turn the heat to high and add the vermicelli, 2 cups of the Stock of Ages, fish sauce, oyster sauce, dark soya sauce and ground white pepper. Season with salt to taste. Stir and detangle the mess of noodles constantly, making sure that each strand is nicely coated in the simmering sauce. If it is getting too dry, slowly add tablespoons of the reserved mushroom soaking liquid, shrimp soaking liquid and stock. Make sure you don't add too much though, as these are fried noodles after all, not soup noodles. Do not overcook, keeping in mind that the noodles will continue to cook even after you remove it from the heat.

Dish out and garnish with as much deep-fried shallots, crackling, green chillies, red chillies and sambal tumis belacan as you want. Serve with whatever deep-fried goodness you've made and relish the silly grin on your face as you realise you've just created one sexy, filthy beast of a noodle dish.

Mee siam is a steaming hot bowl of vermicelli noodles just barely covered with a slightly rich, slightly spicy, slightly piquant, slightly sweet, saucey soup. For me, mee siam evokes memories of primary-school recess time in Singapore. There was a small, family-run stall in the canteen where you could spy different generations behind the counter. It never really occurred to me how many ingredients were required and how laborious this deceptively simple dish was to make until Jason told me exactly what went into it. Afterwards I was convinced that he was either a highly obsessive-compulsive perfectionist or a mentally unstable human being or both. Follow this recipe by Jason though, and you will be greatly rewarded with one of the best street foods ever to come out of Singapore.

MEE SIAM

Saucey Fragrant Soupy Spicy Piquant Rice Vermicelli

FEEDS 4

REMPAH (SPICE PASTE)

14 dried red chillies, soaked in lukewarm water for 1 hour

40 g dried shrimp (hae bee), soaked in lukewarm water for 4 hours, reserving 2 tbsp of the soaking liquid

1 tbsp belacan (dried shrimp paste), toasted (see page 43)

8 shallots, finely chopped

6 candlenuts or macadamia nuts

2 tsp sugar

3 tbsp vegetable oil

3 tbsp tau cheo (fermented soya bean paste)

1 tbsp tamarind pulp

1 tbsp sugar

300 ml coconut milk

300 ml water, plus additional 300 ml

Sea salt

Ground white pepper

100 g Chinese garlic chives (optional)

16 tiger prawns, shelled and de-veined

150 g bean sprouts, tailed

350 g dried rice vermicelli (bee hoon), soaked in hot water for 5 minutes

100 g firm tofu, cut into 2.5 cm strips, deep-fried until golden

2 medium eggs, hard-boiled and halved

2 limes, quartered

Blend all the ingredients for the rempah in a food processor or pound with a mortar and pestle until a smooth paste is formed. Add a drizzle of oil if necessary to help it blend or pound better.

Heat the oil in a wok or large pan over medium heat. Add the rempah and fry, stirring constantly for 8–10 minutes, or until golden brown. Remove the wok or pan from the heat.

To prepare the gravy, transfer half of the rempah to a separate pan and heat over medium heat. Add the tau cheo, tamarind pulp and sugar. Cook for 30 seconds to heat through before adding the coconut milk and 300 ml of water. Bring to the boil and simmer for 30 minutes, or until intensely fragrant and a deep golden brown, and the oil from the coconut milk has separated. Season with salt and pepper to taste. Keep warm over very low heat until ready to serve.

Heat the remaining rempah over medium heat, add 300 ml of water and bring it to the boil. Add the Chinese garlic chives and prawns. Cook for 30 seconds. Add the bean sprouts and rice vermicelli a little at a time and stir to mix thoroughly. Cook for another 2 minutes and remove from the heat.

To serve, place a handful of the rice vermicelli in a bowl. Top with desired amount of tofu and eggs. Pour the gravy over the noodles just before serving and add a gentle squirt of lime.

SHU HAN: I have only a handful of cherished memories of time spent in the kitchen as a little girl with my mum without being chased out to do my homework, and one of the few things I remember making was mee hoon kueh. These handmade noodles are done without any of the faff of a pasta machine or even a rolling pin. The formula is simple, with no egg in it, unlike fresh pasta dough, and I'm sometimes still amazed at the simple miracles flour, water and a bit of bicep work can create. I love mee hoon kueh precisely for its rustic simplicity, down to that egg poached unfussily straight into the broth. I like the mix of crispy saltiness from the anchovies and sweet fragrance from the fried shallots, but you could do with any toppings or extras you like, crudely formed meatballs being one of the more popular options.

MEE HOON KUEH

Singaporean 'Pasta' in a Light Simple Broth

FEEDS 1–2 AS A MAIN
(OR 3–4 AS A STARTER)

100 g all-purpose flour

Generous pinch of fine sea salt, plus additional for seasoning

30 ml water

700 ml chicken stock (page 46)

Ground white pepper

1 egg per serving

1–2 bunches bak choy or other leafy greens, washed and separated

1 tbsp fried shallot oil (page 39)

8 tsp fried shallots (page 39)

8 tsp ikan bilis (dried anchovies), toasted (see page 43)

2–3 stalks spring onions, finely sliced

Light soya sauce, to serve (optional)

Fresh red chillies, thinly sliced, to serve (optional)

Sift the flour and salt together. Add the water and mix. If still too dry, gradually add more water until everything just comes together to form a dough. Knead until soft and bouncy, about 5–10 minutes. Cover with a tea towel or clingfilm and set aside to rest for an hour at room temperature.

Tear walnut-sized pieces from the dough and flatten them between your palms. If you are preparing for a large crowd, you can roll the dough into a flat sheet for faster tearing. Bring the stock to a boil in a large stockpot. Season with salt and pepper to taste. Toss the noodles into the boiling stock. The noodles are ready when they float. Lower the heat and simmer to keep warm.

To poach the eggs, transfer stock from the large stockpot to another pot until half full, and bring to a gentle simmer. Crack an egg into a small empty bowl, then slide it into the hot soup; this additional step is much gentler on the egg and the whites are less likely to wisp away in the soup. Let the egg cook for about 1½–2 minutes for set whites and runny yolks (the only way to have poached eggs). Remove with a slotted spoon and gently transfer to a bowl of cold water to stop the egg from cooking. Repeat with the other eggs and set aside. Just before serving, return the eggs to the stock and heat them up slightly.

Add the bak choy to the large stockpot and turn up the heat to medium. Give the young tender leaves about 1 minute or so to cook, and the larger outer leaves and stems about 2–3 minutes. Reduce the heat to low to keep the stock warm. To serve, top with the greens and a poached egg. Drizzle with shallot oil, and sprinkle the fried shallots, ikan bilis and spring onions on top. Serve with a simple dip of good, traditionally brewed soya sauce and red chillies.

SLURPPPPP

HSUEH YUN

Whenever I get the newspapers in Singapore, I ignore the Sports, Money and Business sections and make a beeline for the Comics section, followed by the Food section. There's always this cheery, bubbly face beaming out of the corner of almost every other food-related column, where she dishes out her recommendations for what's hot and what's not in the overwhelmingly daunting culinary maze of Singapore. That face belongs to Tan Hsueh Yun—and for years, she remained just a disembodied head in CYMK print.

Then I met Hsueh Yun by chance at a vintage café and bakery in Singapore. I had all these ideas that she would be a real diva or a difficult, pernickety, fussy critic, or worse, both, but she could not have been more different. She was warm and friendly and you could see real enthusiasm and excitement in her eyes when she talked about food. One thing led to another and after a flurry of emails, I managed to persuade her to come to one of our dinners when she was travelling in London.

As if having one venerated Singaporean food critic were not stressful enough for the plusixfive team, she brought along one of Singapore's most acclaimed chefs, Willin Low, who coined the term 'Mod Sin' for his modern take on Singaporean food, to our dinner where, coincidentally, the team was doing a modern British take on Singaporean food—cooking Singaporean food with fresh British summer produce. Unfortunately, I was not there when the dinner took place, but by all accounts, the night went swimmingly well and Jason, Shu Han and Christine sure did plusixfive proud.

HSUEH YUN: I'm the food editor of *The Straits Times* and *The Sunday Times* in Singapore. I met the ball of energy known as Goz in a charming cafe called Carpenter & Cook. He offered me a sniff of some artisanal dark soya sauce he had hunted down, and I knew then that we would be friends.

Then I started to get bombarded with information about a Singaporean supper club in London. I was planning a trip to the city and there was a dinner scheduled for the time I would be there. The friends travelling with me asked why I would want to eat Singaporean food in London. I said, well, because they sound crazy and interesting. Why the hell not? We had a great time. I still remember the rabbit satay.

HSUEH YUN: One day an invitation to be in this book appeared in my email inbox. Goz does not take no for an answer, so here's my contribution. Mentaiko spaghetti is one of those easy things you can slap together on short notice and eat out of a large bowl (The recipe makes two servings, but who am I kidding?) in front of the TV before falling gently into a carbo coma. Enjoy.

MENTAIKO SPAGHETTI

Simple and Sinfully Delicious Spaghetti Tossed in Creamy Fish Roe

FEEDS 2

160 g spaghetti

2 sacs mentaiko (marinated pollock roe), 90–100 g

30 g unsalted butter, softened

50 g Japanese mayonnaise

2 tsp rice wine vinegar

4–6 shiso leaves

Handful of nori (dried Japanese seaweed) strips

Bring a pot of salted water to the boil. The water should taste salty like seawater. When it comes to a rolling boil, add the spaghetti. It should take 7–8 minutes to cook.

While the pasta is cooking, slit the sacs of mentaiko down the middle with a sharp knife and scrape out the eggs with a small spoon into a small bowl. Add the butter, mayonnaise and vinegar. Mix well with a spoon and set aside.

Snip off the stems from the shiso. Stack the leaves on top of one another, roll into a tight tube and slice finely crosswise.

When the pasta is al dente, scoop out some of the pasta boiling water and set it aside. Drain the pasta in a colander, shake it a couple of times to get rid of excess water and return the noodles to the empty cooking pot. Add the mentaiko sauce and shiso leaves to the cooked pasta. Mix well with a pair of tongs. If the sauce is too thick, thin it out with a little of the reserved water from boiling the pasta.

Divide the pasta between two serving bowls, top each with nori strips, serve immediately.

YEAH BABY

SHU HAN: Chewy egg noodles, slippery with fragrant lard and fried shallot oil, tangled with minced pork and braised mushrooms, and coated with a crack sauce made with sweet black vinegar, soya sauce and mouth-tingling, spicy sambal. There's a reason why this bowl of noodles is so popular and high on the list of food overseas Singaporeans miss most. If you decide to include pork liver, buying fresh liver is very important, or it will smell of old socks.

BAK CHOR MEE

Noodles Tossed with Mushrooms and Minced Meat

FEEDS 2

100 g minced pork

2 tbsp light soya sauce

1 tsp ground white pepper,
  plus additional ½ tsp

2 bundles fresh egg noodles (mee pok)

Generous pinch of sea salt

3 tbsp Stock of Ages (page 46)

100 g fresh pork liver,
  thinly sliced (optional)

1 tbsp spring onions, chopped,
  to garnish

Fried shallots (page 39), to garnish

Crackling from rendered lard
  (page 44), to garnish

BRAISED MUSHROOMS

4–6 dried shiitake mushrooms

1 tbsp light soya sauce

2 tbsp oyster sauce

1 tsp sesame oil

1 tsp sugar

SAUCE

2 tbsp light soya sauce

2 tbsp Chinese black vinegar

2 tbsp sambal tumis belacan (page 118),
  for a spicy option

2 tbsp tomato-chilli sauce (page 65),
  for a slightly less spicy option

1 tbsp fried shallot oil (page 39)

2 tsp lard (page 44) or vegetable oil

The day before serving, prepare the minced pork and braised mushrooms. Mix the pork with the 2 tablespoons of light soya sauce and 1 teaspoon of ground white pepper. Let sit in the fridge, covered, to marinate overnight. Measure out enough water to cover the mushrooms, then add all the seasonings and mix well. Add the mushrooms and let sit in the fridge overnight to marinate.

The next day, slice the mushrooms into fat slithers and reserve the soaking liquid. Bring the mushrooms to the boil in the soaking liquid and simmer until most of the liquid has been absorbed. The mushrooms should now be plump, and will taste amazing even over plain rice.

To make the sauce, combine the soya sauce, black vinegar, sambal tumis belacan or tomato chilli sauce, fried shallot oil and lard. Divide into bowls.

Blanch the noodles in boiling water until cooked but still al dente. They should still retain a somewhat toothy, springy bite. Drain well and toss hard in a sieve to shake off excess water. Divide into bowls. Dry toss the noodles in the sauce so that each strand is well coated in deliciousness. You can be authentic and let your guests do the mixing themselves after everything is assembled, or be conscientious and do it for them at this stage.

Bring the pork stock to a rolling boil. Season with a generous pinch of salt and the remaining ½ teaspoon of white pepper. Blanch the minced pork in the stock for just 1 minute, or until cooked. Use a fine sieve to remove the pork, then add over the noodles. Repeat with the pork liver.

To serve, top the noodles with the braised mushrooms, crackling, spring onions and fried shallots. Ladle the hot pork broth into four separate small bowls and garnish with an added dash of white pepper and spring onions, then serve with each bowl of noodles.

LARD

SOYA
SAUCE

VINEGAR

HOLY TRINITY OF BCM.

DESSERTS

SHU HAN: It's funny how agar has become the cool new toy for chefs when all along, it's been the kind of jelly Singaporean kids have grown up eating. For the uninitiated, agar is a seaweed-derived substance similar to gelatin, but it sets much more easily at room temperature and gives a bouncier bite. This dessert is often made with coloured agar powder according to the most elementary instructions printed on the packet and set in adorable moulds, so as kids, we loved making and eating these simple treats. I like to use plain, unflavoured agar strands and dye the jelly a natural ruby shade with beetroot. This recipe yields a two-layered agar agar: one a firmer clear jelly, and the other more pudding-like with the addition of coconut milk. Agar agar makes a good dessert for picnics because it won't melt away in the sun. Agar 1: jelly 0.

AGAR AGAR
A Jelly Dessert So Good They Named It Twice

MAKES 20–30

28 g agar strands, roughly cut

1 small beetroot, peeled and chopped

1.5 litres water, plus additional for soaking

2 pandan leaves, tied into a knot

1 cup sugar

Pinch of sea salt

125 ml coconut milk

> TIP: You can get creative with other colours. To make naturally green agar agar, blend or crush the pandan leaves to obtain the green pandan extract. You can also add fruits such as chopped-up mangoes or fresh raspberries. Wait until the second layer of agar has turned semi-firm (about 3 minutes in the fridge) before adding the fruits, so they stay suspended within the jelly.

Soak the agar in a bowl of water for about 30 minutes, or until softened. Drain and squeeze out the excess water. Boil the beetroot in 1.5 litres of water for about 10–15 minutes, or until the water turns deep, dark red. Leave it in longer if you like beetroot.

Add the pandan leaves and agar to the pot and bring to a boil, stirring until the agar has completely melted and there are no lumps. Add the sugar, tasting and adjusting until you're happy with the sweetness. Note that it should be slightly sweeter than you'd normally like it because once refrigerated, it'll taste less sweet.

Remove the pot from the heat. Transfer 375 ml of the agar liquid from the pot to a jug. Add a pinch of salt and stir in the coconut milk (the ratio of agar liquid to coconut milk is 3:1).

Pour the coconut milk mixture into jelly moulds, filling each up to, but not more than, halfway. Alternatively, pour this mixture into a large baking tray with tall sides until it is half full. Transfer the moulds to the fridge, allowing the coconut layer to set until just semi-firm, about 5 minutes, keeping in mind that agar sets really quickly.

Lightly scratch the surface of the semi-set coconut layer with a toothpick so that the next layer can bond to it. Pour the remaining agar liquid on top of the coconut layer up to the brim of the moulds. If it looks like it's starting to thicken and turn lumpy again, just stick the pot back onto the stove to warm it up and stir until it melts again. Refrigerate the moulds until the agar agar is fully set, at least 30 minutes.

To unmould, run a toothpick gently around the edges and flip the moulds over. The agar agar should pop out easily, and in one piece. If you've made them in a tray, cut the agar agar up into your choice of crazy, creative shapes. Refrigerate until ready to serve, preferably cold.

Ask a Singaporean of any ethnicity, and chances are this sweet, multi-coloured snack probably featured one way or another in their childhood. Almost everyone I know eats kueh lapis sagu by cautiously peeling off each coloured segment, making sure not to overstretch and tear the thin, sticky layers. Whenever this is served at the supper club, adults break into chortles and giggles when they see the bright, electric colours. Unable to resist, they are reduced to little kids again, throwing etiquette to the wind as they ignore utensils and peel off the layers with their hands. I won't lie, this is the easiest recipe but it is pretty time-consuming. Every layer requires a good 5 minutes or more of steaming before you ladle on the next layer. So if I were you, I would probably slap on my favourite DVD, turn the telly towards the kitchen and make myself relatively comfortable.

KUEH LAPIS SAGU

Multi-coloured Steamed Cake. Or the Snack That Reverses Ageing.

MAKES 1 (18 BY 18-CM) BAKING TIN

MIXTURE 1
220 ml water, hot
250 g caster sugar
300 ml coconut milk

MIXTURE 2
170 g rice flour
170 g tapioca flour
30 g glutinous rice flour
325 ml coconut milk
170 ml water, room temperature

A range of food colouring

In a large bowl, combine the ingredients for Mixture 1, stirring until the sugar has melted completely. In a separate bowl, combine the ingredients for Mixture 2. Whisk and strain to ensure there are no lumps. Pour Mixture 1 into Mixture 2 and whisk briskly. You want to achieve a nice, smooth batter.

Divide the mixture according to the number of food colourings you have. Add the food colouring, one drop at a time, until you attain the desired shade. I usually divide the mixture into five equal portions (dark red, light red, dark green, light green and plain white). I use only two colours and add fewer drops of it to get lighter shades, but go crazy if you want acid-tripping, psychedelic rainbow colours.

Grease an 18 by 18-cm baking tin. Place the baking tin in a steamer. Spoon a big ladleful of one of the coloured mixtures into the baking tin. Cover the steamer and let that layer cook and stiffen, about 5 minutes. Check by gently prodding the surface with the back of a teaspoon. If it's still gooey, cover and continue steaming. Once the layer is firm, pour another ladleful of a different coloured mixture and steam. Repeat with each colour until the tray is full or you run out of mixture. Do not be tempted to add the next layer until the previous layer has completely solidified! The more layers you add, the longer it takes. The top layer may take up to 10 minutes to stiffen completely.

Let the kueh lapis sagu cool down to room temperature before refrigerating for at least 2 hours. This allows the kueh lapis sagu to set properly and aids in the unmoulding process. To serve, slice with a clean knife dipped in warm water. Clean the knife before every slice. Then stand back and watch in amusement as kids and adults alike become four-year-olds again.

We had this delicious, gooey, buttery cake on the menu of our April Fool's dinner listed as a petit four called 'Roast Pork'. Throughout the dinner, the guests were scratching their heads, wondering why the heck a savoury dish of pig was being served as dessert after Milo ice cream. Probably due to my hyperactive imagination, I've always thought that this dessert's dark, golden-brown crunchy top resembles the crispy crackling of roast pork. Kueh bingka ubi is incredibly easy to make and will definitely excel beyond any realm of spectacular if you can find and grate fresh coconut and tapioca. Do not despair or hang your head in shame if you can only find frozen coconut and tapioca though—it'll still work pretty darn well anyway. No one will judge you. Promise.

KUEH BINGKA UBI

Baked Tapioca Cake

MAKES 1 (30 BY 30-CM) BAKING TIN

455 g tapioca, grated

2 large eggs

120 g unsalted butter

225 g brown sugar

240 ml coconut milk, plus additional 3 tbsp

1 tsp sea salt

Preheat the oven to 190°C. Place all the ingredients, except for the 3 tablespoons of coconut milk, in a microwaveable bowl. Cook it in the microwave on high heat for 3 minutes. (There is no shame in using a microwave. Be brave, be strong. If you don't have a microwave, you can combine the ingredients in a pot over a stove, but you'll need to stir the mixture constantly, watching it like a hawk to ensure that it does not burn.) Stir to evenly combine all the ingredients.

Cook the batter in the microwave on high heat for 3 more minutes. Stir again. The bits at the side of the bowl should start to firm up at this point; just stir the stubborn bad boys back into the batter. Continue to microwave on high heat in 3-minute intervals, stirring between each one, until the batter achieves a fairly thick and gloopy consistency; it should take a total of about five intervals. At this point, the batter should resemble oat porridge or thick, runny honey.

Line a baking tin with parchment paper and pour in the batter. Bake in the oven for about 45 minutes, or until a skewer comes out clean. Brush the top with the remaining 3 tablespoons of coconut milk. Turn the oven to its grill setting and bake again until the top turns dark golden brown, watching it like a hawk as the top can burn easily depending on how powerful your oven is. Let cool on a wire rack before slicing into desired shapes.

This Malay dessert was served at a supper club called 'No More Mr Rice Guy', where we decided not to serve any rice. Despite howls of protests and evil eyes from Shu Han, I decided to sneak in kueh lopes as a dessert for a little ironic twist. (I'm not sure she has forgiven me yet.) When invited for a meal by a Malay household, it's a classic rookie's error not to save some stomach space for the amazing array of desserts often served at the end of a heavy Malay meal of curry and rice and all manner of heart-stoppingly rich side dishes. This is one of those desserts—delicious and, unless you make a concerted effort to do so, pretty darn difficult to cock up.

KUEH LOPES

Steamed Glutinous Rice Cakes Drizzled with Palm Sugar Syrup

MAKES ABOUT 15

6 pandan leaves, lightly scraped
    with a fork and tied into a knot;
    plus additional 4 leaves, lightly scraped
    with a fork and tied into a knot

300 ml water

500 g glutinous rice

15 banana leaves,
    cut into 7.5 by 25-cm strips

2 tsp sea salt

250 g fresh desiccated coconut, to serve

GULA MELAKA SYRUP (MAKES 1 CUP)

1 cup gula melaka (palm sugar)

½ cup water

The day before serving, boil the 6 pandan leaves in a pot with 300 ml of water for 30 minutes over high heat. Remove the leaves. Let the water cool down to room temperature, then transfer the pot to the fridge and let sit until cold. Soak the glutinous rice in the cold pandan water overnight. Soaking aids in the cooking process, giving the rice grains better bite and infusing them with the flavour of pandan.

The day you are serving this dessert, soak the banana leaves in hot water for about 15 minutes, or until soft. Fold each leaf so that one half crosses over the other in a *V*-shape, forming a small cone in the middle. Fill the cone with 3 tablespoons of glutinous rice. Then fold down the two halves and wrap the ends around the glutinous rice cone tightly. Gripping the rice parcel tightly together, use string to tie the leaves securely so the parcel doesn't explode or leak during boiling.

Fill a large pot two-thirds full with water. Add the remaining 4 pandan leaves and salt, and boil over high heat. When the water comes to a rolling boil, add all your bondage kuehs. Boil them for 1 hour, then remove and let cool.

Meanwhile, to make the gula melaka syrup, bring the gula melaka and water to a boil. Lower the heat and simmer until the syrup is thick enough to coat the back of a spoon.

Unwrap the kueh lopes and serve with a generous drizzle of gula melaka syrup and a dusting of desiccated coconut.

TIP: I sometimes cheat by adding a few drops of pandan essence when pandan leaves aren't readily available. The only problem is that pandan essence colours the rice a bright, lurid Incredible Hulk green, which may be a tad shocking to some.

This is one of the first dishes I learnt how to make from my mum. It was my first party trick and every time my mum had a dinner party, I was tasked with making it. I was 10 years old when I learned the recipe, and it sure as hell was not because I was some sort of chef prodigy, but because it's so bloody simple to make. If you can boil water, you can make this. This is a traditional recipe, but for a modern twist, we have served round discs of sago, added a dash of sugar, blowtorched the top so it resembles a crunchy crème brulee, and added a quenelle of gula melaka ice cream. Finish off this dessert with a swirl of coconut milk and more gula melaka (palm sugar).

SAGO GULA MELAKA

Tapioca Pearls with Coconut Milk and Palm Sugar Syrup

FEEDS 4

250 g tapioca pearls (sago)

4 pandan leaves, scrunched up and tied into a knot

300 ml coconut milk, warmed up with 1 tsp of sea salt, to serve

GULA MELAKA SYRUP (MAKES 1 CUP)

1 cup gula melaka (palm sugar)

½ cup water

Wash the tapioca pearls and soak them in cold water for at least 1 hour. Wash and rinse again after soaking. Transfer the tapioca pearls and pandan leaves to a pot, and cover with enough water so that the water level is at least 4 cm above the pearls. Bring the water to a boil, stirring constantly so that the pearls do not clump together or worse, stick to the bottom of the pan and burn. Stir for about 5–10 minutes, or until the pearls start to turn translucent, then immediately remove the pot from the heat and strain with a large, fine-mesh sieve. Run the sieve under cold water, using a chopstick to stir the pearls gently, which will cool them down and get rid of excess starch.

Fill any receptacle you want to serve the pearls in, or a container or mould in the desired shape if you intend to unmould the pearls. Let sit in the fridge until it's properly cold, about 2–3 hours.

Meanwhile, to make the gula melaka syrup, bring the gula melaka and water to a boil. Lower the heat and simmer until the syrup is thick enough to coat the back of a spoon. Let cool and refrigerate until ready to serve. (Don't worry, it won't solidify after being refrigerated).

To serve, unmould the chilled sago (or leave it in the container if you wish) and drizzle with copious amounts of gula melaka syrup and coconut milk.

JASON: I have very fond memories of these chewy, delectable balls, my favourite Peranakan kueh of all time. I used to spend many of my childhood days making these alongside my nan and she would always make sure these were available whenever I visited. So when I announced my debut at plusixfive, I knew right away that these would have to be featured on the menu. These are usually served warmed so when you bite into them, you are greeted with a river of warm, oozy gula melaka (palm sugar). These were so well-received that for my second supper club, I invented my own modern take on this traditional kueh. There was a drink that I used to have as a child called bandung, made with rose syrup and evaporated milk. So I decided to utilise this familiar flavour and turn the normally green ondeh ondeh into balls of pink yumminess. And I am rather glad to say, those went down a storm too.

ONDEH ONDEH

Glutinous Rice Balls Exploding with Warm Oozy Palm Sugar

MAKES ABOUT 30

20 pandan leaves, cut into small pieces

500 ml water

450 g glutinous rice flour

1 tbsp caster sugar

350 g gula melaka (palm sugar), finely grated

150 g fresh desiccated coconut

Blend the pandan leaves and water in a food processor until a green pureé is formed. Strain through a sieve to remove the pulp and reserve the pandan juice. Combine the glutinous rice flour, caster sugar and pandan juice in a large bowl. Knead lightly to bring the flour mixture together into a soft dough.

Pinch a small piece of dough and roll it into a ball, no bigger than the size of a ping pong ball. Flatten the ball into a disc and make an indentation in the middle with your thumb. Fill with a teaspoon of grated gula melaka and roll it in your palm to form a smooth ball, sealing the filling inside. (If the ondeh ondeh is not well-sealed, the palm sugar will explode and ooze out during boiling.) Repeat with the rest of the dough and gula melaka.

Bring a large pot of water to the boil and add the ondeh ondeh. Boil for 3–4 minutes, or until the ondeh ondeh float to the surface. Remove from the pot with a slotted spoon and roll in the desiccated coconut to coat. Serve immediately.

TIP: To make the desiccated coconut taste even better, add a pinch of salt and spread evenly on a plate, then steam for 20 minutes. This useful tip comes from a lady who used to run a hawker stall selling ondeh ondeh!

BONUS: To make bandung ondeh ondeh, substitute the pandan leaves and water with 200 ml of rose syrup, 150 ml of water and 1 teaspoon of red food colouring. Mix the rose syrup, water and red food colouring and use in place of the pandan juice.

Traditional min jiang kueh is soft, pillowy and cake-like, while its distant, trendy, flimsy-ass cousin resembles a thin, crispy wafer. No prizes for guessing which one I prefer. There is something heart-warming about walking home from school in 33°C heat, waiting in line in a horribly humid hawker centre, and then sinking one's teeth into a steaming hot, fluffy pancake, inevitably dribbling a shower of crushed peanuts all over oneself and grinning like a happy fool with peanut and sugar crumbs smeared all over one's teeth. To make the aromatic peanut filling, the peanuts are first toasted until they give off a rich, nutty aroma. The addition of the lightly toasted sesame seeds provides a subtle fragrance. It's important to use granulated sugar and not fine caster sugar, as the large sugar crystals will add to the contrasting, and more importantly, satisfying crunch which you are trying to achieve here. This was adapted from a recipe by Jason.

MIN JIANG KUEH

Soft and Fluffy Peanut Pancakes

FEEDS 4–6

FILLING

400 g raw peanuts, toasted (see page 43), skins removed and roughly chopped

150 g granulated sugar

75 g white sesame seeds, toasted (see page 43)

1 tsp sea salt

PANCAKES

600 g all-purpose flour

2 tsp baking soda

2 tsp dry yeast

1 tsp sea salt

300 g granulated sugar

3 large eggs, lightly beaten

850 ml water, lukewarm

Mix all the ingredients for the filling in a large bowl and set aside. To make the pancake batter, sieve the flour, sugar and baking powder together in a large mixing bowl. Add the eggs and water, then mix thoroughly with a whisk or fork until the batter is smooth. Cover loosely with a damp tea towel or cling film, and let it rest in a dark and warm place (if you are in Singapore, that's any cupboard space) for the yeast and baking soda to get busy and for the batter to double in size. This should take about 1½ hours.

Heat a non-stick frying pan over medium heat. Lightly grease the pan with a little bit of vegetable oil. Pour a big ladleful or about 120 ml of the batter into the frying pan so that it covers the bottom completely. Cover with a lid and cook for 5–6 minutes over medium-low heat, or until little bubbly craters start to form, and the top looks nice and dry and there are no wet splotches. The pancakes should be a light shade of brown.

To be honest, your first pancake is likely to be a failure as you try to get the hang of it and figure out the appropriate amount of heat to apply. Chances are you will get too impatient and try to remove it from the heat too quickly. But don't fret! There is truth in the age-old adage that practice makes perfect!

Gently remove from the pan in one piece and lay flat. Spoon as much filling as you want onto one half of the pancake. I love the filling, so I always generously pile on the peanuty goodness, but 2–3 tablespoons should do it. Fold each pancake in half. Slice into quarters or wedges and serve immediately.

LEIGH

Like a few of the other guest chefs featured in this book, I first met Leigh when she came to my supper club. Leigh is one half of the culinary duo Two Hungry Girls. She also runs her own company, craftcakes, where she holds baking and cake-decorating classes and painstakingly churns out custom-designed cakes. Leigh has made gravity-defying, topsy-turvy Alice in Wonderland cakes, furry Muppet monster cakes and my favourite, a cake that looks exactly like a massive pork pie. Leigh is professionally trained and has worked in some of the best pastry kitchens in New York and London. We've worked together for a few events as I've always found her desserts to be absolutely gorgeous. The way she deftly marries distinct Asian flavours with Western techniques always astounds and surprises me.

LEIGH: Having grown up and lived in Singapore for most of my life, I was spoilt by the great number of high-quality Chinese and Singaporean eateries around. Great food at affordable prices was such a given in Singapore that I never learnt how to cook until I went abroad to study. But I sorely missed the familiar tastes of home, and only then did I learn how to cook. Fast forward a couple of years. After I obtained my pastry arts diploma from culinary school in New York, I moved to London.

It was there that I met Shuwen through a mutual friend, and we immediately clicked through our incessant talk about food. She subsequently quit her corporate job and moved to Beijing for eight months to learn Chinese, and it was there that she promptly fell in love with the food, language and culture.

At the same time, back in London, I was just discovering the supper club scene and plusixfive was the first supper club I ever went to. I loved the food, the atmosphere and the idea of feeding a bunch of strangers in your own flat, with a menu decided by the chef! I met Goz and once he learnt that I was a pastry chef, we promptly started talking about a collaboration. In true Goz style, nothing is as straightforward as it seems, and I ended up making the bread course, main dessert and petits fours for one of his private events. It all went swimmingly well and marked the beginning of a foodie friendship and various other collaborations.

Upon Shuwen's return to London, we decided to start our own supper club featuring creative Chinese cuisine that combined our Southeast Asian heritage with Mainland Chinese cuisine. With my training as a pastry chef, we also placed plenty of importance on stunning desserts, a course often neglected in Chinese cuisine. With that, Two Hungry Girls supper club was born. The kopi tart has amassed a small cult following among supper clubbers in London and it was one of the first few desserts we created for the supper club.

LEIGH: These moreish tartlets were first dreamed up when I wanted to create a dessert version of the strong coffee sweetened with condensed milk, or kopi, so commonly found in coffee shops in Singapore. I created these for our Two Hungry Girls supper club and we've since had many people asking for the recipe. Like cups of kopi, these tartlets come with a thin, sweet layer of condensed milk hidden under the coffee jelly, providing a sweet counter to the coffee jelly's bitterness. The best way to eat them is to pop a whole tartlet into your mouth! It's like downing a powerful shot of sweet coffee encased in a malty biscuit—the perfect ending to a meal.

KOPI POP TARTS

Horlicks-flavoured Tarts with Sexy Bursts of Bitter Coffee and Condensed Milk

MAKES 20

HORLICKS PASTRY
(MAKES ABOUT 500 G OF DOUGH)

225 g all-purpose flour

25 g Horlicks powder

190 g unsalted butter

75 g demerara sugar

30 g egg whites

2 g sea salt

1 cup hot espresso or strong
  instant coffee

3 tbsp granulated sugar

2 tbsp water, cold

1 tsp powdered gelatin

300 ml double cream

2 tbsp caster sugar

1 sachet 3-in-1 instant white coffee

Condensed milk

To make the Horlicks pastry, sift the flour and Horlicks powder together and set aside. Beat the butter and sugar with an electric mixer until pale and fluffy. Add the egg whites and beat. Add the flour mixture and salt, and beat until a soft dough is formed. Let sit in the fridge for at least 2 hours.

Preheat the oven to 180°C. Break off pieces of dough and press them into small canapé-sized tartlet moulds. Bake for about 15 minutes, or until golden. Let cool completely on a wire rack and store in an air-tight container until ready to use.

To make the coffee jelly, pour the hot coffee into a small bowl, then add the sugar and stir until fully dissolved. In another small bowl, add the cold water, then add the gelatin and allow to soak for 5 minutes. Add the gelatin mixture to the hot coffee. Let sit in the fridge until set, about 2 hours. The jelly will be very soft, dissolving into liquid coffee once it hits your tongue.

To make the coffee cream, beat the double cream with an electric mixer until you see light streaks form. Slowly add the caster sugar and half a sachet of coffee powder to the mixture. You can add the whole sachet if you prefer your coffee cream stronger. Continue beating until soft peaks form. It is important not to overbeat the cream at this step or you will get butter instead of silky, light coffee cream.

To assemble the tarts, spoon a very thin layer of condensed milk into each tartlet shell. Spoon a small teaspoon of coffee jelly over the condensed milk and top with a dollop of coffee cream. Alternatively, use a disposable piping bag fitted with a small star nozzle and pipe a swirl of coffee cream onto each tartlet. Voila!

Some of the textures of the desserts we make, while they might seem normal to Singaporeans, are just a tad too peculiar for some. Too often have we had non-Asian guests scrunch up their faces at being served 'hot sweet gloopy rice congee' (pulut hitam) or sweet potato soup. It's completely counter-intuitive for a culture which serves soup as a starter and porridge for breakfast. Don't even get me started on things like glutinous rice cakes (muah chee), which I've heard being compared to everything gross imaginable, from glue to bodily fluids. Ice cream has been my way of attempting to make Singaporean desserts slightly more accessible and familiar to Westerners, since ice cream is practically a universal dessert. We have made everything from teh tarik ice cream to coconut and gula melaka ice cream. It also allows us to be slightly more creative and make cheffy, pretty plated desserts (we think). Once you get a hang of the basic recipe and method, feel free to experiment with other flavours! Virtually anything can be ice-creamised, I reckon. So go on, and get those creative, designer-y juices flowing!

BASIC ICE CREAM RECIPE

MAKES 1 LITRE

Egg yolks from 4 medium or 3 large eggs

200 ml whole milk

175 g light brown sugar

1 tsp sea salt

600 g double cream

Beat the egg yolks and set aside. Heat the milk, sugar and salt in a saucepan over low heat until the milk begins to steam, stirring constantly to ensure the sugar melts evenly. Drizzle 2–3 tablespoons of the steaming milk onto the egg yolks, whisking as you go along. Slowly pour the egg yolks into the saucepan containing the milk. Stir the mixture slowly and continuously over low heat until it forms a custard thick and creamy enough to coat the back of a spoon. Strain the milk custard through a sieve into a large bowl containing the double cream, and discard any lumps. Stir well to combine. Let cool and refrigerate for a few hours or preferably overnight. When removed from the fridge, it should be cold to the touch. Churn in an ice cream maker according to the manufacturer's instructions.

COCONUT ICE CREAM

Substitute 200 ml of coconut cream for the whole milk and follow the basic ice cream recipe. When churning in the ice cream maker, add 100 g of lightly toasted desiccated coconut (see page 43) at the end as it churns. Serve with our classic pulut hitam (page 234), or for a pretty little shake-up, spoon a puddle of black glutinous rice on a plate, add a quenelle of coconut ice cream, sprinkle some toasted glutinous rice, and drizzle on gula melaka syrup.

VANILLA ICE CREAM

Scrape the seeds of two vanilla pods into the saucepan containing the milk, sugar and salt, then heat over low heat and continue with the basic recipe. If you're feeling like something simple, serve with fresh strawberries, or as part of Dave's Pineapple, Rum, Vanilla recipe (page 232).

GULA MELAKA ICE CREAM

Substitute 200 g of shaved gula melaka (palm sugar) for the light brown sugar and follow the basic ice cream recipe. For a refreshing variation on our classic sago gula melaka recipe, shape the sago into little round discs using a mould or cookie cutter. Spread a layer of fine sugar on each disc. Using the oven at a very hot grill setting or a blowtorch, caramelise the sugar and leave it in the fridge to set. This creates a crunchy contrast to the soft sago. Serve with a quenelle of gula melaka ice cream and a drizzle of gula melaka syrup.

TEH TARIK ICE CREAM

In a saucepan over medium heat, steep 10 strong Assam tea bags in the milk. Turn off the heat just after it comes to a boil. Let the tea bags steep and infuse for at least 2–3 hours. (I like the flavour of the tea to be quite strong and slightly astringent, so I tend to use a couple more tea bags and let it infuse for a longer time.) Remove the tea bags, add the sugar and salt and reheat over low heat, continuing with the basic recipe. For a twist on prata—that classic Singaporean midnight supper or post-clubbing snack—roughly tear up fresh, piping hot prata, sprinkle sugar, and add a dollop of teh tarik ice cream.

CREAM

MILO ICE CREAM

Substitute 100 g of light brown sugar and 100 g of Milo powder (pure powder, not 3-in-1) for the light brown sugar in the basic recipe. If you want your ice cream richer, add more Milo. Follow the basic ice cream recipe. When churning in the ice cream maker, add 3 heaped tablespoons of Milo powder as it churns. To create the lovechild of Singapore's version of the ice cream sandwich and a Milo Dinosaur, the ubiquitous drink served in Malay and Indian hawker stalls, lightly toast small, thin slices of brioche, add a quenelle of Milo ice cream to each toasted slice, dust liberally with Milo powder and lightly drizzle on condensed milk.

DAVE

Whenever I used to hear the word 'barbecue', all that came to mind was uncooked, burnt meat and cold beer. But, that was before I met Dave in the heady summer of 2012, when he had a little barbecue makeshift pop-up called Burnt Enz under the railway arches of East London. An alumni of Asador Etxebarri, the Basque restaurant which earned its Michelin star by using the most basic and primal methods of cooking—simple smoking and grilling over an open fire, Dave never used charcoal but relied on wood chips, and he'd handmade these brick ovens which weighed over two tonnes and spat out fire at 800 degrees celsius. He also had a primitive Victorian-looking contraption with hand cranks and pulleys that lifted and dropped whatever he was cooking onto smouldering hot coals. You had to be Colonel Kurtz crazy to be working with these bad boys. Or you had to be Dave. Every time we went to Burnt Enz, he kept banging out a procession of smoked and grilled delicacies. But after the summer was over, just like Keyser Söze, he upped and disappeared. Grabbed his bags and went backpacking. I thought I would never see that dude again. Then one day, he told me he'd been offered to head up a restaurant in Singapore called, unsurprisingly, Burnt Ends. It might be a spankingly posh restaurant now and quite far removed from the 'plastic tables under tattered beach umbrella' look of London's Burnt Enz, but the food he churns out still takes me back to the blinding summer of 2012 and spending too much time under those arches. Life sure has a strange way of making sure I am fed well.

DAVE: I met a blonde-headed Goz when he came and ate at my summer residence, Burnt Enz in East London. I ended up in London working at St. John Bread and Wine, The Loft Project and Viajante, after stints at Tetsuya's, Noma and Etxebarri. After hearing too many good things about his plusixfive supper club, I went down to see what it was all about. Awesome Merlion food in London. I then headed off to travel in South America, hitting up Venezuela, Colombia, Ecuador, Peru and Bolivia. After a phone call with a couple of hospitality legends, I found myself relocating to Singapore to open up Burnt Ends Sg instead

of heading back to East London. Who would have thought, that within four months of eating at Goz's supper club, I would find myself indulging in Singaporean food permanently. Goz has been a great help with my transition to Singapore, with his extensive network of friends, contacts and places to eat. It just so happens, that one of the restaurants Goz was inspired by, Blue Ginger, is across the road from my house and round the corner from my restaurant. Singapore is a great hub to be in—plenty of amazing chefs, great all-night hawker food and a perfect base for making cheeky eating holidays!

DAVE: I liked the idea of doing a pineapple dish because we're in a region where pineapples are grown. I had done a roasted pineapple in London with Ben from Lucky Chip to make the ultimate Hawaiian pizza and it was amazing. So I thought we could turn it into a dessert! When I think pineapple, I think rum, so pineapples and rum with a smoky twist was the dessert I came up with.

PINEAPPLE, RUM, VANILLA

FEEDS 8

Vanilla ice cream (page 228)

RUM SYRUP

300 g dark brown sugar

200 g water

30 g dark rum

2 vanilla pods

5 black peppercorns

ROASTED PINEAPPLE AND CRISPS

1 pineapple

Water, for sugar syrup

Caster sugar, for sugar syrup

FRENCH MERINGUE

125 g egg whites

125 g caster sugar

125 g icing sugar

GARNISH

100 g pistachios, toasted

Fresh baby mint leaves, washed

Make the ice cream and rum syrup well before serving to allow the ice cream to set properly and the rum to infuse. You can make the syrup beforehand and refrigerate to keep.

To make the rum syrup, combine all the ingredients in a pan over low heat and bring the temperature to 100°C. Remove from the heat, let cool to room temperature and strain.

Preheat your oven or barbeque to 230°C. Peel the pineapple and cut it in half crosswise. Roast it in the oven or barbeque for between 1 hour and 1 hour 45 minutes, rotating or flipping several times until cooked through and a nice smoky crust has formed. Remove from the oven and let cool.

Turn down the oven to 120°C. Make sugar syrup out of equal parts water and sugar; bring water to a boil and dissolve sugar completely, stirring constantly, then remove the pan from the heat. To make the crisps, slice the top half of the pineapple thinly. Dip the slices of pineapple in the sugar syrup. Bake in the oven for 30–45 minutes. Remove, let cool and set aside.

To make the French meringue, whip the egg whites and caster sugar until soft peaks form. Sieve the icing sugar and fold in. Bake in the oven at 100°C for 1 hour 45 minutes. Remove, let cool and set aside.

To serve, cut a 1-cm thick slice of the roasted pineapple. Remove the core of the pineapple and warm gently in the oven. Roughly chop the toasted pistachios and crush the French meringue. Combine and generously spoon over the pineapple ring. Add a scoop of vanilla ice cream and a good couple of spoonfuls of the rum syrup. Stick the pineapple crisps in the ice cream and garnish with baby mint leaves.

SHU HAN: Bubur pulut hitam is a traditional porridge dessert made with black glutinous rice and served with lashings of coconut milk. Black rice is very high in antioxidants, but this tastes way too good to be dismissed as bland health food, especially after it's been given a plusixfive twist. This black sticky rice pudding is heaven in a bowl: warm, chewy, little amaranth grains, sweetened with the delicious, toffee-like flavour of gula melaka (palm sugar), fragrant and crisp toasted coconut flakes, and the best part—that ripple of rich, ice-cold coconut ice cream running and melting through it all.

BUBUR PULUT HITAM

Warm Black Rice Pudding with Coconut Ice Cream

FEEDS 5–6

1 cup black glutinous rice

5 cups water, plus additional
   to replenish

½ cup coconut milk

Pinch of sea salt

½ cup gula melaka (palm sugar),
   plus additional to taste

GULA MELAKA SYRUP (MAKES 1 CUP)

1 cup gula melaka (palm sugar)

½ cup water

TO SERVE

Coconut ice cream (page 228)

¼ cup fresh desiccated coconut,
   toasted (see page 43)

Soak the rice overnight in cold water. The next day, you should find that the grains have expanded. Drain and rinse well. Don't try to be smart or lazy by skipping this step—not soaking the rice will mean an extra couple of hours of cooking, and unevenly cooked rice at that.

Bring the rice, 5 cups of water and coconut milk to a boil in a large pot over high heat. Decrease the heat to low and simmer for about an hour, or until the rice is soft and cooked; stir once in a while so the grains don't settle to the bottom of the pot and burn, and replenish the water as needed so that the rice is submerged while cooking. At the end, most of the water should have evaporated and the rice should resemble porridge. Turn off the heat.

Add the salt and stir in the gula melaka until it dissolves, then remove the pot from the heat. Season to taste with more gula melaka or salt. Err on the side of sweetness, with a hint of savouriness.

To make the gula melaka syrup, bring the gula melaka and ½ cup of water to a boil. Lower the heat and simmer until the syrup is thick enough to coat the back of a spoon. Let cool.

To serve, scoop the rice into bowls and serve warm with a generous scoop of coconut ice cream, a sprinkle of dessicated coconut and a drizzle of gula melaka syrup.

YUM

(sorry.)

SO, YOU WANNA START A SUPPER CLUB?

When plusixfive turned one, I wrote a guide on our website about how to start a supper club. In our first year, London's foodie and supper club scene exploded, and suddenly it seemed like there was a new supper club popping up every other week. Most of them seemed to be Asian-themed and set up by people who were generally annoyed that their nation's cuisine was being under- or mis-represented, watered down, or anglicised, in London. All these supper clubs brought a smile to my face and I thought, why not share some tips, rants, whines and grumbles we've had or learnt along the way? No one else should have to make the same dumbass mistakes we did.

I was also encouraged to write this guide by emails or forum posts from overseas Singaporeans who'd heard about plusixfive and who wanted to know why there wasn't a similar supper club in their country and were inspired to start one. So this one's for you kiddos—the Rosetta stone of supper club secrets. I hope you read this, rock out the patriotism and the Majulah Singapura, bring some badass Singaporean food action to wherever you are and kick some taste buds into action.

1. Money, Money, Money

If you're starting a supper club because you wanna make a heck of a lotta money from it, then stop reading now. Unless you own your own farm and rear your own poultry or cattle, chances are you'll probably be going to your local supermarket to buy groceries, and so you're already losing out on profit margins as you're not getting your produce directly from the source. Then take into account the amount of time, energy and elbow grease that goes into each supper club dinner, all that time spent prepping and cooking and cleaning and washing up, the broken plates and cups (you're bound to get at least one uncoordinated, clumsy or drunk guest), scratched-up pots and pans, overworked dishwashers and not to mention that evil scum of the earth—last-minute cancellations. Truth be told, running a supper club is not really worth the money, but that's not why you're doing this, right?

2. Legal Schmegal

Before you start daydreaming about your James Beard award-winning supper club idea, take the time to look up the various laws in your part of the world relating to alcohol and restaurant licensing, health and safety, insurance and occupier's liability. The whole concept of supper clubs in some countries straddles a dreadfully grey area of the law, as they are not licensed as restaurants and accordingly are not subject to the various standards and licenses required of a restaurant. Some supper clubs get around this by accepting payment only in the form of 'suggested donations'. They also do not sell any liquor, at the risk of being slapped with a violation of liquor licensing laws. This is why most supper clubs are BYOB. You can also talk to other supper club owners, but most importantly do your own research. Just because other people are doing it doesn't make it legal.

3. Think of a Novel Idea or Concept

What are you trying to showcase? Think of an interesting and novel concept, or a cuisine that you are so crazy passionate about and that you've actually got the skillz to cook. I think it's a fair assumption to say that people going to a supper club are usually going because they actually want to eat reasonably good food.

And for goodness' sake, think of a concept or cuisine that hasn't been done to death. There's probably a gazillion supper clubs out there in London touting themselves as English supper clubs. So think of how you can differentiate yourself from the pack. Have a theme. Or be the supper club that cooks recipes from *The Fat Duck Cookbook* (hm...you heard it here first).

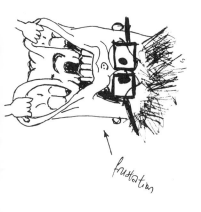

frustration

4. Help Out at a Well-reviewed or Well-respected Supper Club

See firsthand how a good supper club is run. It'll be even better if you can get a supper club to let you help out so you can really get into the thick of it and see how it's all run operationally. It's a win-win situation for all. You'll probably get to eat the food, interact with guests and generally have a rocking good time. And at the end of it all, you can decide if you still want to set up your own supper club—or you might end up thinking, "WHAT KIND OF MAD PSYCHOS WOULD DO SHIT LIKE THAT TO THEMSELVES! I'D RATHER SELF-FLAGGELATE!"

5. Come Up with a Catchy Name

Need I say more? Put some thought into it, for crying out loud. You want people to remember your supper club, right? For some reason, plusixfive has turned out to be a surprisingly difficult name. People seem to keep spelling it wrongly. We have seen 'plusfixfive', 'plussixfive', 'pusfixsive' etc. and we have had people look at our business cards and mumble "plooooo-six-five?" or "plooos-eeks-five"... Sigh, you get the idea.

#duckyeah
#nakedbodie
#glovesonbab

6. Dealing with Your Landlord

Yes, I'm boring and risk averse, but if you're renting, it's best to check with your landlord if he minds you hosting a supper club. Some landlords couldn't give a hoot; but some might care a lot and use it as an excuse to terminate your lease. Check your tenancy agreement. Alternatively, get your landlord drunk and make him sign a waiver.

7. Cleanliness Is Next to Godliness

If you need me to tell you this, then you probably shouldn't be allowed to feed people. You definitely don't want some enraged, botulism-stricken diner suing your sorry ass because you couldn't be bothered to wipe down your kitchen properly, decided to double-dip the tasting spoons or use that dented tin of sardines which was way past its sell-by date. Despite not being subject to proper licensing and health and safety standards by law, you should definitely adhere to the appropriate standards.

8. Fix a Date

You will talk and talk for ages about hosting your first supper club dinner. But nothing's going to happen until you fix a date for the first session

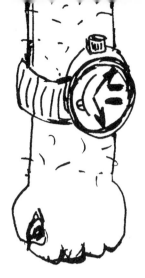

or trial. Then figure out how many people can comfortably fit into your home, and how many you can reasonably cook for. You don't want to stress yourself out for the first one. Once you have fixed a date and committed to it, invite a whole bunch of friends, foodie types, family, enemies, superheroes and villains. If you know influential people, you should probably invite them as well.

9. Social Media Is Your Friend

I don't profess to know the ins and outs of social media, but a fellow Tweeter summed it up when, in a rare moment of sobriety and cruel bluntness, he screamed, "Dude, without Twitter, plusixfive would be nothing!" After crying my eyes out and curling up into a foetal position while sucking on my thumb, I figured that he was probably right. Twitter and all those friends I've made on it have really helped plusixfive out a *huge* bunch. I cannot think of a faster way to get the word out on the street about your new venture and if it's good, people *will* talk about it. It's the best word of mouth monster ever. (But I guess it works both ways, so conversely, if your supper club is crap, you are screwed.)

And if you do sign up for a Twitter account, for the love of God, try to be interesting. Yes, people come to a supper club for the food but they also come for the experience, so if you're as boring as drying paint, no one's gonna come. Well, no one interesting or sane anyway.

10. Planning and Timing

Sit down one day and list all the dishes you think you can cook competently and confidently. Now take that list and split it between (a) what can be done very quickly (for example, salads, cut fruits, gazpacho, oyster shooters) and (b) what needs days of prepping (for example, beef rendang). You want to achieve a good balance between the two. Ideally you want to be able to prep *everything* beforehand and then just reheat or assemble or flash fry during service. But unless you are serving nothing but stews and salads, that's going to be pretty difficult. Assuming you aren't a professional chef armed with an industrial kitchen and a legion of sous chefs, you want to be able to dish out starters that you have prepped beforehand and maybe just require some simple assembly. Then whilst people are gobbling that up, you can go on to prep your next dish.

Time yourself. You don't want too much lag time between the courses as people absolutely hate waiting for their food. Guests don't like to be rushed either, so don't throw everything on the table in the first 20 minutes.

Here's a fairly typical plusixfive dinner schedule.

7.30PM: Guests arrive.

8PM: I usually serve up three starters, which I've prepped beforehand and which need minimal reheating or grilling. Starters are served in reasonably small portions and they usually go quite quickly, so you have to keep an eye on your guests and make sure they don't get too bored while waiting.

8.15PM: Meanwhile, I prep the mains. I might, for example, spoon out something I made earlier in the day or the night before, like my beef rendang or my chap chye or fish head curry. Then I'll serve up the rice and mains. Now these are pretty big-bum dishes so everyone's going to sit back and chillax and pace themselves for the meal. Also because there's rice, everyone's going to chill out and eat it slowly. Well—most of the time anyway. Here you'll usually get some time to mingle and talk about the dishes. You might also have to top up the rice because people sometimes ask for more.

8.45PM–9PM: This is when there's usually some peace and quiet in the kitchen. So I churn out a quick and easy item on the menu, usually frying an egg dish, which is pretty easy, or a prawn dish because prawns cook quickly.

9.30PM: I leisurely serve up my desserts and coffee, thanking my lucky stars that no one stabbed themselves in the face with chopsticks or choked on a fishbone.

In a nutshell, plan dishes you can cook and serve with a reasonably quick turnaround. You might want to show off all your crazy cooking skills and people might appreciate the effort, but they will also curse you and your family vehemently when they have to leave at 3am in the morning. This is made worse in a supper club because if a dish is taking too long in a restaurant, you can just tell the waiter to cancel the order and leave. But in a supper club, generally nice human beings won't leave, or they'll feel it's too awkward to leave, and this ruins the general dinner vibe.

11. Utensils

This sounds stupidly obvious, but for the love of God have enough plates, cups, utensils, napkins and placemats. In fact, have more than enough. For utensils and crockery, you can hit up IKEA, where they do some seriously nice and simple Scandinavian-looking plates. I get all my utensils and crockery from thrift stores or antique fairs for a bargain.

In general, no matter what the theme of your supper club is, you should ensure that:

A. Everyone has a clean set of plates and cups, and that there are sufficient utensils and serving spoons, carving knives etc.

B. There should be spares lying around in case something breaks, or if someone drops a spoon and isn't quick enough to adhere to the five-second rule. And there will inevitably be that one person who keeps losing his cup and coming round to ask you for another. Or that dude who needs three different glasses to drink three different beverages from.

There's another good reason for being well-stocked with crockery and utensils. Neither you nor your guests want you to be stressing out, washing and drying plates halfway through dinner. It slows everything down and you lose momentum, your guests get bored, they can't leave because it's awkward, they're obliged to stay, you stress out even more, serve bad, burnt or undercooked food, they want to leave even more but can't because it's awkward...Everything is thrown out of whack.

12. Bums on Seats

Unless you regularly have large numbers of people in your house or your buttocks have a burning desire to sit on a different seat every day, chances are, no regular person owns enough chairs for a supper-club dinner.
I recommend buying foldable plastic stools from IKEA or, if you're in the UK, from Argos. Cheap and functional, you can fold them up when the dinner is over and hide these anti-design monstrosities out of sight. I advise getting them way ahead of time. I once had stools delivered to me on the morning of a supper club, and they all arrived broken. All four of them. Lesson: Never leave anything till the last minute. Duh.

13. Pricing

Don't be an idiot and charge stupid amounts for your supper club, especially if you aren't a well-known chef or supper club. Go find out what others are charging and hover around that price. If you go above that, you'd better justify it by serving pot loads of seafood or just be plain freaking amazing.

14. Final Tip: Enjoy Yourself and Be Super-Epic-Party-Rocking-Hard

Your guests vibe off you. So if you aren't vibing, they aren't *vibing*.
People go to supper clubs not just to eat the food. Chances are they came for the food AND also to interact with the chef, the front of house, to ask about the food, talk to other guests, or learn about the cooking. They came because they wanted a fuller, more fun, and wholesomely rounded experience than going to a restaurant. They didn't come to cheer you up if you were having a bad day or couldn't get it together.

So on the night itself, enjoy yourself, turn up the AC/DC, Spice Girls, PJ Duncan or whatever gets your booty shaking and your guests vibing. Think Big Vibes. Like Ad-Rock from the Beastie Boys said, you gotta "rock the house party at the drop of a hat yeaaaaaaaah!" Now, go forth my young Padawan and give your guests one helluva good time.

GOODNIGHT AND GOOD LUCK

When this whole shindig of a supper club started on a cold, grey evening in London on 29 May 2011, it was just me feeding 10 good friends in my tiny little flat.

I never in my wildest dreams imagined that it would turn into what it is today.

What it has grown into.

I never thought we would get mentioned in newspapers in the UK, Hong Kong, Malaysia, Ireland and Singapore, or that I would end up feeding over 50 people in a Victorian building in South Kensington, London, hawking laksa in a farmers' market in Hong Kong, or be invited to panels and on live television to discuss hawker food in Singapore, or that one day I would be compiling all our recipes and stories into this very cookbook.

More importantly, I never imagined that plusixfive would grow into a motley crew of equally, if not more, crazed and obsessed foodies willing to sacrifice their weekends to run plusixfive with me.

Most of all, I'd like to thank everyone who came to our dinners and warmed the *hum* (cockles) of my heart.

You now hold in your hands every dirty little secret of plusixfive, and as everyone's favourite uncle once said, "With great power comes great responsibility", so get out there, cook, learn, experiment and feed someone!

THANKS

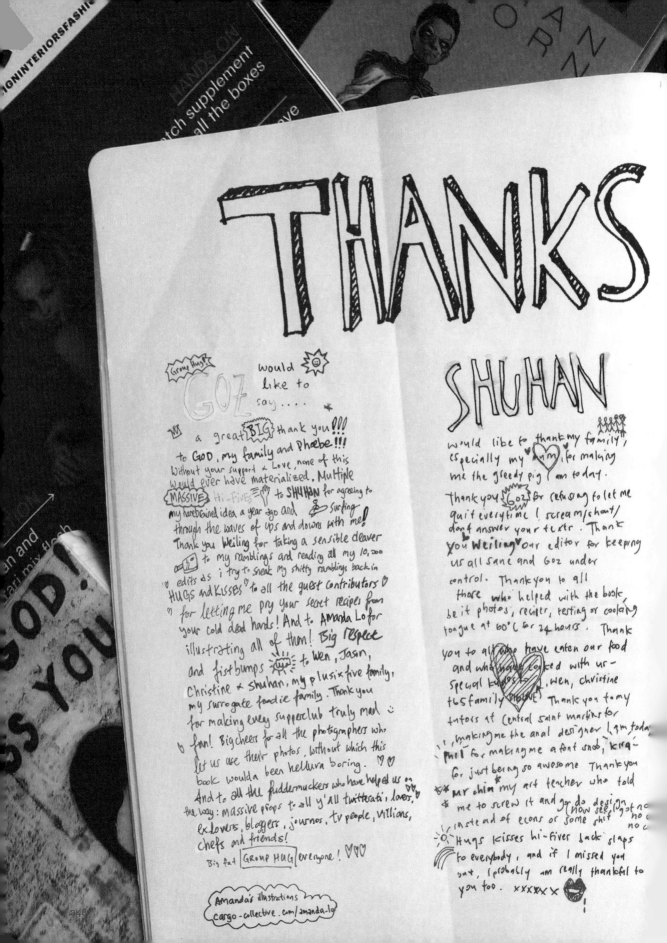

Group Hug! **GOZ** would like to say....

a great BIG thank you!!! to GOD, my family and Phoebe!!! Without your support & Love, none of this would ever have materialized. Multiple MASSIVE Hi-fives to SHUHAN for agreeing to my harebrained idea a year ago and surfing through the waves of ups and downs with me! Thank you Weiling for taking a sensible cleaver to my ramblings and reading all my 10,000 edits as i try to sneak my shitty ramblings back in HUGS and KISSES to all the guest contributors for letting me pry your secret recipes from your cold dead hands! And to Amanda Lo for illustrating all of them! Big respect and fistbumps to Wen, Jasin, Christine & shuhan, my plusix five family, my surrogate foodie family. Thank you for making every supperclub truly mad fun! Big cheers for all the photographers who let us use their photos, without which this book woulda been helluva boring. And to all the fuddruckers who have helped us on the way: massive props to all y'all twitterati, lovers, ex.lovers, bloggers, journos, tv people, villians, chefs and friends!

Big fat GROUP HUG everyone!

Amanda's illustrations cargo-collective.com/amanda-lo

SHUHAN

would like to thank my family, especially my mum, for making me the greedy pig I am today. Thank you Goz for refusing to let me quit everytime I scream/shout/ don't answer your texts. Thank you Weiling our editor for keeping us all sane and Goz under control. Thankyou to all those who helped with the book, be it photos, recipes, testing or cooking tongue at 60°C for 24 hours. Thank you to all who have eaten our food and who have cooked with us — special guests, Wen, christine the family. Thank you to my tutors at Central saint martins for making me the anal designer I am today, Phil for making me a font snob, Kira for just being so awesome. Thank you mr chin my art teacher who told me to screw it and go do design now see I got no taste instead of econs or some shit no no Hugs kisses hi-fives back slaps to everybody, and if I missed you out, I probably am really thankful to you too. xxxxxx

A TINY INDEX

Sorry, why do I have to write in this book? You guys fucking rock, you don't need me to tell you that. OK, here's my review – awesome, as usual. Can I go back to my bee now? Thanks

Sam xxx

Jow! Mummy I can cook can cook! Amazing food, glorious portions, stuffed – really stuffed!